The Real Food Chef

2012

RFC

The Power of Plant

Dr Libby

Facebook.com/DrLibbyLive

@DrLibbyLive

Pinterest.com/drlibbylive

Dr Libby Weaver

Dr Libby

Dr Libby Weaver

Disclaimer

The contents of this book are for information only and are intended to assist readers in identifying symptoms and conditions they may be experiencing. This book is not intended to be a substitute for obtaining proper medical advice and must not be relied upon in this way. Always consult a qualified doctor or health practitioner. The author and publisher do not accept responsibility for illness arising out of the failure to seek medical advice from a doctor. In the event that you use any of the information in this book for yourself or your family or friends, the author and the publisher assume no responsibility for your actions.

Printed in China.

First Printed in 2012

Published by Little Green Frog Publishing Ltd

Revised Edition

Little Green Frog Publishing Ltd
www.littlegreenfrogpublishing.com

www.littlegreenfrogpublishing.com

ISBN: 978-0-473-29816-6

Dr Libby's Real Food Chef

The Real Food Chef 2012 RFC

The Power of Plant

Dr Libby

DR LIBBY WEAVER WITH CHEF CYNTHIA LOUISE

For all of the precious people
who have wanted to amp up
their greens but haven't known how...

This is for you.

My mission is to educate and inspire,
enhancing people's health and happiness,
igniting a ripple effect
that transforms the world.

— Dr Libby

Contents

Snacks

Dinner

Sauces

Dessert

Extras

The Real Food Chef Cooking System

Nutrition is one of the most debated topics in the health arena. People are constantly looking at new ways they can improve their nutrition and subsequently their health but unfortunately they are often misinformed.

Theories around the healthiest way to eat are circulating everywhere. After noticing my clients were struggling with ideas for quick and nutritious high-plant meals, it seemed a natural progression to provide a series of recipes with my seal of approval after the incredible interest shown in my best-selling books *Accidentally Overweight* and *Rushing Woman's Syndrome*.

I knew the recipes had to appeal to a broad range of people from busy mothers to teenage boys to anyone wanting to maximise the nutrition in their diet. That concept soon evolved into providing optimal nutrition to the masses. Good, honest food that could be made by anyone. These recipes are sure to impress even the fussiest of eaters. Nutrient-dense but still packed full of flavours. *The Real Food Chef* (RFC) recipes are supported by the addition of animal protein if desired.

The protective benefits of a mainly plant-based diet have been recognised by a vast number of scientific studies, most famously and comprehensively in the findings of the China Study. Science supports the immense health benefits conferred by a high-plant diet due to numerous mechanisms, one of which is the immensely positive effect this way of eating has on blood chemistry.

The Real Food Chef system focuses on using organic food in its whole form including all of the foods' vitamins and minerals and the natural plant compounds known to support human health... after all, it is nutrients that keep us alive. The recipes are all free from refined sugars and dairy products and they are gluten-free with a few exceptions, which use spelt flour. This can be easily substituted for good-quality gluten-free flours. *The Real Food Chef* recipes are therefore suitable for those with some of the more common food allergies or intolerances.

The Real Food Chef concept is a dynamic combination of my nutritional expertise and one of Australia's leading organic and whole-food chefs, the passionate Chef Cynthia Louise. I have guided and approved each step in the creation of the recipes, always with my mission statement, my driving force in mind: My mission is to educate and inspire, enhancing people's health and happiness, igniting a ripple effect that transforms the world.

I want to enhance people's nutritional intake in a way that is practical for them. One of my signature concepts is the *Real Food Chef* seal of approval. If you eat 35 times a week, made up of 3 main meals and 2 snacks, and if currently 7 of those 35 meals meet my criteria for a health-enhancing, nutrient-dense meal, then creating just 3 RFC meals per week will take your intake to 10 out of 35. For most of you, that will feel very simple and it will also be delicious! If you then decide that adding 3 RFC meals per week over a month was simple, you may add another 4 the next month, which would take your total to 14 out of 35 meals in a week. That means that in two little months out of your very long life, you have doubled your nutrient intake. Talk about health-enhancing! Unless a complete overhaul of your pantry and essentially your life appeals to you (which if it does, go for it!), gradual changes will be far more sustainable for you and/or your family.

If you begin to focus on taking great care of your physical health, a huge part of that means taking care of the way you feed yourself.

It is very difficult to be kind, compassionate and patient with others, as well as yourself, when you are filling yourself with stimulants and food that contains very little, if any, nutritional value. Think about that.

The Real Food Chef recipe system covers breakfast to dinner and everything in between, including some delicious and decadent desserts. It also contains the reasons why I am suggesting you transition to the *Real Food Chef* way of nourishing yourself. As I like to say, "When you know your what and your why, the how shows up." *Real Food Chef* contains the what, why and the how and it will revolutionise the way you nourish your body, mind and soul.

Increasing the Nutrient Content of the Diet Through a High-Plant Diet

A health-enhancing diet is a diet based on plant foods. Incorporating more plant foods into your diet is the quickest and easiest way of increasing the nutrient density.

Plant foods are good sources of soluble and insoluble fibre. Insoluble fibre helps provide bulk to our stools to keep our bowels regular and is used to help feed our gut bacteria. Feeding the good bacteria is an essential component of keeping the balance between the good and not-so-good bacteria in the gut. A healthy digestive system is the foundation of good health. It is all very well to be consuming a nutrient-dense diet but if your digestive system is not absorbing and utilising these vitamins and minerals you will not reap the benefits.

Nutritionally, leafy greens are superstars. They not only contain vitamins and minerals but they enhance the quality of your blood. They also contain amino acids, which are the building blocks of our proteins. In your body, amino acids make up the cells of your immune system that help defend you from infections and cancer; they create the neurotransmitters that influence your mood and they build your muscles that drive your metabolic rate and give you your physical strength. The power of greens is demonstrated in the way gorillas live and given that they are similar to humans from a DNA perspective but have not been influenced by marketing, we can learn a lot from their innate food choices. The diet of gorillas is over 50 percent piths, shoots and green leaves and yet they have one of the highest muscle masses of any living creature and are very strong. They eat some animal protein, which they obtain mostly from insects, but the ratio of greens to animals is enormously in favour of a high-plant diet.

Green leaves are also alive. Our bodies thrive on being supplied with living foods so the more we can incorporate plants into our diet the better we feel. One of the main reasons plants accumulate nutrients is to develop future seeds so they can reproduce and so that the species can survive. Seeds require a high density of nutrients to fulfil their reproductive functions. Even once they have germinated they need a significant amount of energy and nutrition to sprout and survive. For this reason, you will notice that we have added these nutrient-packed powerhouses called sprouts to many meals.

Plants accumulate nutrients long before they create their seeds and there is no better place for accumulating and storing nutrients than in the leaves. Hence greens leaves are one of the most nutritious foods on Earth. Seeds too are rich in nutrients but plants don't want their "offspring" to be eaten, so many plants also add protective mechanisms to their seeds by endowing them with a range of inhibitors, alkaloids, and other substances that may be harmful to "predators". Nature is truly amazing.

If you grow greens or herbs yourself, the best time to harvest them is before the formation of seeds. This is when the green leaves have the highest concentration of nutrients. After a plant blossoms, nutrients begin to accumulate inside the seeds and once the seeds are gone there is almost no nutrition left in the leaves. They tend to turn yellow and dry out and fall off — think of a parsley plant after it has gone to seed — so that the remaining nutrients return to the soil and the plant can rest until the next growing season. Seasons and cycles in nature all serve a purpose and human health relies on these cycles to nourish and sustain our life.

Supporting Optimal Blood pH by Providing Practical Ways to Include More Green Vegetables in Meals

The pH of your blood is always alkaline, but before we go any further on this topic that is so crucial for people to understand when it comes to their health, here's a quick refresher on pH from high-school chemistry.

The acidity or alkalinity of any solution is determined by how much hydrogen (H+) and hydroxide (OH-) ions are within the substance and this is expressed as pH, meaning "power of Hydrogen" (or 'potential of Hydrogen'). The pH of a solution is a mathematical calculation based on a scale from 0 to 14, where 7 is neutral. This is the pH of distilled water, where the relative concentrations of H+ and OH- are equal. For every unit below pH 7, the concentration of H+ increases by a factor of 10. Those kinds of solutions are acidic. For every unit above 7, the concentration of OH- is increased similarly. Those kinds of solutions are alkaline.

Your blood is always alkaline. It is held within a very narrow range with 7.365 being ideal and your body will work very hard to keep you here. However, the foods and liquids you consume every day have a significant effect on the pH of your blood. Most high-water vegetables and some fruits including lemons have an alkaline effect on blood pH while meat, dairy and most cereals are more acid-yielding.

A lemon, though very acidic in itself, will actually reduce the body's acidic load once its mineral contents are absorbed into the blood. This is because the predominant minerals within the lemon (for the science-minded among you, these are the electrically positive cations of calcium, potassium, sodium, and magnesium) have an alkalising (acid-reducing) effect on blood chemistry. They do this by forming mineral hydroxides and carbonates in our cells, which act like molecular sponges to "soak up" excess acidity.

There is much debate about the diets of our ancient human ancestors and the precise ratio of animal to vegetable matter they consumed. What is known is that for outstanding health, the effect of animal food on blood chemistry, if it is eaten, must be buffered by a higher quantity of plant foods that push blood chemistry to the more alkaline end of the spectrum. That way our blood is happy and our health can be optimal.

What we also know is that since the industrial revolution around 180 years ago (it occurred over a lengthy time frame), most people's diets have become much more heavily dependent on foods that push our blood chemistry to the acid end of the spectrum and our bodies have not been able to adjust. The industrial revolution didn't just mean the beginning of railways and sewing machines, but also the processes of canning, refining sugars and milling flour, which led to an unprecedented shift in the human diet. As people began to eat in this "progressive" way, choosing more and more "convenience" foods, they significantly reduced their intake of wholesome whole foods, particularly green vegetables, replacing them with more white flour and more white sugar than had ever been consumed before throughout all of human history. When the human diet is based on highly processed foods that are virtually devoid of all nutrients, health will suffer.

I am often asked: if our diet is, in general, so lousy, how is it so that people tend to be living longer these days in the Western world? My answer to this question is a question: are we living too short and dying too long? It is the quality of life that I care about so passionately. In the second half of your life you do not want to lose your independence and have to rely on another person to do up your shoelaces because you can no longer reach them because you are so stiff. You don't want to have to go to hospital every second day to be hooked up to a dialysis machine because your kidneys can no longer clean your own blood. Yes, genes play a role. Of course they do. But we need to remember that the health choices we make today influence which genes will be switched on now or in the future as well as how we will feel and function both today and in the future.

LET THAT EMPOWER YOU TO KNOW THAT YOU CAN SIGNIFICANTLY DECREASE YOUR RISK OF DEVELOPING SOME OF THE MAJOR DEGENERATIVE DISEASES IN OUR WORLD ALONG WITH POSITIVELY INFLUENCING THE QUALITY OF YOUR LIFE BOTH TODAY AND IN THE FUTURE SIMPLY BY CHOOSING A HIGH-PLANT, NUTRIENT-DENSE DIET.

As mentioned above, it is critical that the pH of human blood stay as close as possible to 7.365 (slightly alkaline). If it drops below 7 (acidemia) or rises above 7.8 (alkalemia), coma and death can quickly follow. Consequently, the human body does everything in its power to ensure that the pH of its tissues remains within stringent confines.

For example, to preserve pH balance under conditions of chronic acid load (as occurs with a diet high in processed foods and alcohol), the body must continually draw on its alkaline reserves by releasing calcium, potassium, and magnesium from the bone matrix to neutralise excess acid. In addition, the body begins to break down muscle protein in order to release the amino acid glutamine. In turn, glutamine is converted to glutamic acid (glutamate) by the liver and, in doing so, it binds with excess hydrogen ions and ammonia is generated. The ammonia is then excreted in the urine, along with chloride ions that are needed to balance the electrochemical charge.

If all of that sounds too scientific, all you need to know is that eating too many foods that push your blood to the acidic end of the spectrum will drive your body to release minerals that are alkaline in their nature from their storage houses, the bones, into the blood to even out the effects of the acid. That way the blood is happy but your bones have been thinned in the process. I personally believe this is one the major reasons why we see so much osteoporosis in the West compared with those eating a traditional Eastern diet, which is based mainly on plant foods, and little or no processed food.

Amp up your greens for outstanding bone health as that way your body will not need to call on your bones to release their precious minerals to counterbalance the effects of an overly acidic lifestyle. Your muscles will also love you by preventing the progressive muscle wasting that can come from an overly acidic diet. Given your muscles significantly influence your metabolic rate, your ability to utilise carbohydrates for energy, and your strength, they are worth maintaining or preferably building.

The pH of our blood is also believed to influence the body's ability to burn body fat or store it. The best way to imagine it is that every cell in the human body is bathed in blood (plasma) and when the pH is ever-so-slightly too acidic, the cells hold onto additional fat to insulate themselves from the "acid burn". So a way of eating that fosters alkalinity also serves your body's ability to burn body fat as a fuel.

In addition to facilitating the development of osteoporosis and, in some cases, an increase in body fat, an acid-promoting diet initiates a broad cascade of biochemical and physiological changes to our chemistry that can damage our health.

These include: chronic oxidative stress, enhanced catabolism (muscle wasting and destruction of skeletal reserves), elevation of insulin and cortisol (both linked to body-fat storage and a host of other biochemical effects as described in *Accidentally Overweight*), systemic inflammation, and impaired immunity. Each of these situations has its own documented adverse health effects... just imagine the implications when they are all happening at the same time! Let it empower you to know that a high-plant diet can have a significant impact on the prevention of these undesirable biochemical states and hence such a wonderfully positive and powerful effect on your quality of life.

The Difference Between Digestion Acidity and Blood Alkalinity

It can be confusing when you hear about the importance of acidity in the digestive system and the importance of alkalinity in the blood. When it is said like this, it is clear they are two distinct systems. As mentioned in the digestion section ahead, having optimal acid levels in the stomach is essential for effective digestion, both in the stomach itself, plus to set up the pH gradient as the digestive tract continues. If the acid in the stomach is not acidic enough, the food will not be broken down correctly, and partially undigested food will end up too far along the digestive tract. If this occurs, that food is fermented, and this drives undesirable gut bacteria to take up residence in the colon. These bacteria often make lactic acid, which further impairs digestion, nutrient absorption, and liver function, as well as adding additional acid to the body's load. Poor digestion has an acidifying effect on blood chemistry, a significant reason why it is so important to optimise this process.

Decreasing the Synthetic Chemical Load Being Consumed by Encouraging the Use of Organic Food

Decreasing the synthetic chemical load is another important aim of the Real Food Chef way of eating. Eating more organically or biodynamically grown food or simply choosing spray-free options can play a major role in achieving this.

When it comes to pesticides, it is my opinion that we are guinea pigs when it comes to the long-term consumption of these substances. The reason a conventionally grown apple looks so perfect is because it has been sprayed to make it that way. We cannot see or taste the chemicals on its skin, but they are there. Pesticides have to be tested before they can be used on food for human consumption. However, they are often tested for such a relatively brief amount of time. I do not believe we can compare tests done over, say, a six-month period to being exposed to these substances over an entire lifetime. What also cannot be tested is what happens when the chemicals are mixed, and they get mixed inside our body every day when we eat conventionally grown produce.

Fresh food the way it comes in nature is an incredibly important part of our diet.

Please do not be scared off from eating a conventionally farmed apple. I simply want to encourage people to choose organic produce whenever they can. Also, think about the way you eat the food. We peel a banana. It may have been sprayed, but how much gets through the skin? We actually don't know. But surely there would be less chemical residue in the flesh (inside) of a banana than on the skin. So perhaps choosing a conventionally grown banana is not too bad. No one really knows. Yet, when it comes to an apple, we usually eat the whole fruit. So you would be better to choose an organic (or biodynamically grown) apple wherever possible.

Think about this. Organic food is the true cost of food. I once started and ran an organic café. Once a week, a local farmer delivered fresh greens picked that morning from his biodynamic farm. I always set aside some time on the day of his delivery to chat with him, as he always had wonderful tales to tell of life on his farm. One day, when I asked him how he was, his reply was along the lines of "not so good". When I enquired further, he went on to tell me that snails had invaded his broccoli patch, virtually overnight. When I paused to consider this, I realised that, if they took hold, a portion of this man's meagre livelihood would be lost. So I asked him how he deals with snails on his broccoli given that his farming principles do not involve spraying the patch to get rid of the invaders (which would have taken less than thirty minutes to do).

My farmer friend went on to tell me that snails lose their "stick", their ability to suction on to things, in salty water. So he made up a bottle of salt and water, and he spent two days, crouched down on all fours, crawling between his broccoli plants, squirting saline water up under the fronds. Not only that, he didn't kill the snails, he collected them in a bucket and fed them to the chooks "to keep them in the food chain" as he so delightfully put it.

Think about each of these scenarios. Spray in under thirty minutes versus crawling around on your haunches for two days. For me, that illustrates precisely why organic and biodynamic food costs more. It reflects the real cost of food, plus many foods grown this way have a greater nutritional value. The more of us who choose it, the cheaper it will become. Every time you spend money, you are casting a vote for the kind of world that you want. The more we demand organic and say no to chemicals, the more organics will have to be supplied. I know I'm on my soapbox, and I want to remain real and practical with the advice I offer. In simple terms, choose organic food whenever you can.

If organic food is simply not available in your area or it is too costly for you to buy, try this solution to remove pesticides. Pesticides tend to be fat-soluble and general washing does not remove them. Washing food can remove dirt and germs, but not most pesticides. To wash food for both dirt and pesticides at the same time, fill your sink with three parts water to one part vinegar, and wash your fruits and vegetables. Then rinse them in fresh water, pat them dry, and store them for use. Do what is practical for you.

Furthermore, plants have innate mechanisms designed to help them protect themselves from pests. When a plant is left to grow of its own accord and not sprayed with pesticides, the plant creates substances within itself to help ward off pests. These substances, however, don't just have the ability to help protect the plant; they are substances that often behave as antioxidants when humans consume them. And if the plants are sprayed, they no longer have to (and don't) produce these substances that enhance human health. So eating organic food is not just about what you miss out on (pesticides) but also what you get (more antioxidants).

Pesticides typically have to be altered inside the body before they can be excreted. The liver is one organ involved in this process. The liver has to prioritise detoxification processes and if there are more liver loaders present than available pathways for this to occur, the pesticides are usually stored in the fatty tissue of your body. Hence when any weight-loss process is undertaken, liver support is of immense importance.

Do what you can to decrease the synthetic chemical load in your life by also considering what you put on your skin. You only have to think about how nicotine patches work to realise that your skin is a direct route to your blood supply and that your detoxification systems will have additional work to do. There are some beautiful skincare companies out there who create highly effective products that contain zero synthetic ingredients. In my ideal world

you would be able to eat your skincare.

On another note, some herbicides contain compounds that can mimic estrogen in the human body, in both males and females of all ages. This is of great concern. For estrogen itself or estrogen-like compounds to exert their effects they have to bind to estrogen receptors and when they do, the lovely or not-so-lovely effects of estrogen are felt. Given that children today are exposed to herbicides for their entire lifetimes, it is likely that their exposure to additional estrogen-like compounds (additional from what the body makes itself, mostly from puberty onwards) is contributing to the earlier age of menarche being reported across the Western world. Pause and consider the ramifications of this.

Decrease your regular intake of synthetic chemicals by choosing organic produce or growing some of your own food, such as herbs, wherever you can. However, if this overwhelms you then don't start here. Come to this when you are ready. In the meantime focus on enhancing your detoxification processes, discussed in the next section, to upregulate your body's ability to excrete these substances.

Enhancing and Supporting Detoxification Processes

Another reason to eat The Real Food Chef way is to enhance your body's ability to detoxify itself. Detoxification is a process that is often misunderstood. It is a process that goes on inside us all day, every day. We wouldn't be alive without it. However, it is the lifestyle choices we make that influence how efficiently our body is able to detoxify.

The liver plays a major role in detoxification, which is essentially a transformation process. The body takes substances that if they were to accumulate, would harm you, and changes them into substances that are less harmful so that you can excrete them.

Substances that influence detoxification processes include alcohol, caffeine, synthetic substances, including medications, pesticides and ingredients in skincare, trans fats (damaged fats usually found in bought cakes, biscuits and muesli bars) and refined sugars. The liver also has to detoxify substances your body makes itself such as estrogen and cholesterol.

One of the goals of the *Real Food Chef* recipes is to firstly eliminate the "liver loaders", allowing the body to pull stored toxins out of storage to be processed and excreted. For example, the first stage of detoxification by the liver requires B vitamins for that process to occur. Our best food sources of B vitamins are whole grains and yet many people have cut them out or certainly right back in this high-protein era we are currently living through. Many people feel better without them (or with less or only specific types in their diet) and I am by no means suggesting you suddenly go back and eat bucketloads of grains to get your B vitamins

Food is designed to supply the body with the nutrients necessary for the detoxification processes in the body to work efficiently.

if you feel better without them. All I want to point out is that unknowingly, people can miss out on nutrients crucial to the inner workings of their body and for optimal health.

Choosing a wide variety of whole foods, and perhaps trying some gluten-free grains, if gluten-containing grains disrupt your digestive system, may assist these vital cleaning systems in your body. Eating the Real Food Chef food also helps with regular bowel motions and this too enhances detoxification processes as the liver no longer has to pick up the shortfall of digestion. The liver loves and is stimulated by bitter foods and there is no better way to stimulate the bitter taste buds than with greens.

Supporting the Energy Systems of the Body Through Optimal Nutrient Intake

When I ask people how they are, these days I most often hear "exhausted", "stressed", "busy", "frantic", "broken" and "tired". I don't want this for you. I want you to feel amazing. I want you to feel energised, vital and alive.

Without energy, it is difficult to make your own dreams come true and contribute to those around you. How do you wake up in the morning? Do you bounce out of bed, grateful that a new day has dawned that you are blessed to be part of? Or do you press snooze six times wondering how on earth it can be morning already? Mostly I hear the latter.

What is your energy like over the course of the day? Do you feel like your blood glucose is more akin to a roller coaster, with dramatic highs and lows that are represented in your moods, than the even flow of a river? When you have a burst of energy does your temper explode or do you simply wish you could spend the next year in bed? My point? Your energy levels significantly influence the quality of your life.

Food is designed to energise us in a lovely, even way. If what you've been eating makes you want to go to sleep then it hasn't been serving you. Eating the *Real Food Chef* meals is designed to help support the energy systems in your body and this is one of the mechanisms through which it does.

The concept of photosynthesis may not be something you've considered since high school. Yet it is a process essential to life. Photosynthesis is a process used by plants (and other organisms) to convert the light energy captured from the sun into chemical energy that can be used to fuel the organism's activities. Diagrammatically it looks like this:

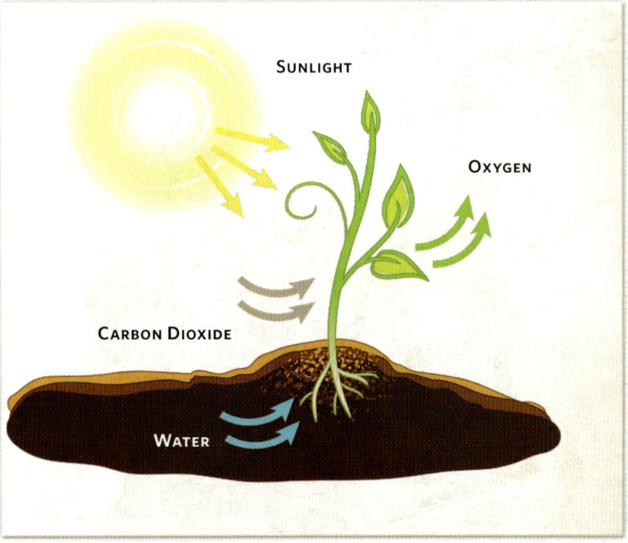

Green leaves are the only living thing in the world that can transform sunshine into energy, in a food that living creatures can consume. Hence why one of my favorite catchcries is, "Amp up your greens — it's like eating sunshine."

Knowing this, it is hard to imagine how there could be life on Earth without greens. They produce chlorophyll, which, put simply, is liquid sunshine. Chlorophyll has powerful health properties of its own. In fact haemoglobin, a component of human blood that helps transport oxygen around the body, is almost identical to chlorophyll.

All of the energy in food comes from the sun. Think about this every time you eat your greens and amp up their content in your diet to enhance your energy systems.

The way energy is actually created within the body involves a cascade of biochemical pathways that nutrients drive. I had them pinned all over the walls of my bedroom while I was at university. I shan't bore you by pinning them inside our cookbook! Just know that by increasing the nutrient-density of your diet, you help enhance your energy systems, which can lead not only to a healthier life but a much happier one too.

Digestion: the Foundation of Optimal Health

When making changes to optimise your health, improving your digestion is a key place to start. We all know it is best to build your house on a strong foundation, and building a robust digestive system is much the same.

Gut issues have become widespread with over 70 percent of women in many Western countries reportedly suffering from Irritable Bowel Syndrome (IBS). You only have to look at the amount of advertising targeted at improving gut health to see the prevalence of this problem. Improving digestion can have the most profound effect on your overall health and with simple, easy steps you can make radical change.

The first step to take when wanting to improve your digestion is to chew your food well. There are no more teeth to chew your food once it has left your mouth! A little strange, you may be thinking, but so many of us are in such a hurry with our meals or we are so excited by the flavour of our food that we might chew each mouthful four times if we're lucky. We tend to inhale our food. Instead, slow down and chew. Do whatever it takes to do this. Engage in conversation. Put your fork down between each mouthful. Chew your food and swallow it before you put the next mouthful in. Observe whether this improves how your tummy feels after eating.

Once food has been somewhat broken down in the stomach, it moves through the pyloric sphincter, a one-way valve leading into the duodenum, which is the beginning of the small intestine. Physically, in your body, this valve is located in the middle (or just slightly on the left) of the chest, just below where a lady's bra sits and just below a man's pectoral muscles.

While food is in the stomach, messages are being sent to the pancreas to secrete sodium bicarbonate (as well as digestive enzymes), which has a highly alkaline pH. The bicarbonate is designed to protect the lining of the first part of the small intestine as well as to allow digestion to continue.

What is known as a "pH gradient" is established all the way along the digestive tract, and each region of the big long tube has an ideal pH. When the pH gradient is not established in the stomach, that is, when the pH is higher than ideal, digestion problems are likely further along the tract. These may be symptoms of the small or large intestine, such as bloating, pain, or excessive wind. It also means that the absorption of nutrients may be compromised. Insufficient pancreatic bicarbonate production may also cause digestive symptoms such as a burning sensation underneath the stomach in the valve area described above. Pain in this area can also indicate that the gall bladder needs some support or investigation. It is best to consult with your health professional about this if you feel discomfort in this area.

The best way to let the pancreas know that it needs to jump to action and produce bicarbonate and digestive enzymes is to have good stomach-acid production at optimal pH. The digestive system runs off a cascade of signals from one organ or area to the next, via the brain. Use the suggested strategies that follow, and remember to chew food well, to stimulate the pancreas to fulfil its role.

The small intestine is where absorption of most of the nutrients in the food you eat begins. As food moves through the small bowel, digestive enzymes are secreted not only by the pancreas but also by the brush border (lining) of the small intestine. The role of these enzymes is to continue what the stomach acid began, which is to continue to break down the food we have eaten into its smallest, most basic components. It is in the small intestine that you absorb most of the goodness (vitamins and minerals) from your food.

All of the goodness, all of the nutrients that keep you alive are drawn out of your food and into your blood so that your body can use those nutrients to do all of the life-sustaining jobs they do. Alcohol and vitamin B12 are virtually the only substances you absorb directly out of your stomach (rather than your small intestine) into your blood. Alcohol tends to be in your blood within five minutes of consuming it, which is why humans may get tipsy if they drink it on an empty stomach.

For the most effective digestion, we need the pH of our stomach acid to sit around 2. Water has a pH of 7 (neutral pH) or above, depending on the mineral content (the higher the mineral content, the higher/more alkaline the pH level). When you add a liquid with a pH of 7 or more to one with a pH of 2, what do you potentially do to the stomach acid? You dilute it. And we need all of the digestive fire we can

muster to get the maximum nourishment from our food and the best out of us. So, in my ideal world, we wouldn't drink water thirty minutes either side of eating.

Stomach acid is stimulated by chewing, the aroma of food, as well as by the consumption of lemon juice and apple cider vinegar (ACV). The chewing action sends a message to the stomach to let it know that food is on its way. When we inhale our food, this doesn't happen. Historically, we regularly took much longer to prepare our meals and the slow cooking processes generated an aroma of the upcoming meal, again signalling to the stomach that food was on its way. Nor was there as much adrenalin

constantly zooming about in our veins, drawing the blood supply that typically supports digestion away from these processes to the periphery (arms and legs), priming you for your pending escape from danger, which is what adrenalin prepares you for.

Lemon juice and ACV physically stimulate the production of stomach acid. If you haven't consumed either of these before, it is best to initially dilute them and ideally consume them five to twenty minutes before breakfast (or all of your main meals if that appeals). For example, you might begin with half a teaspoon of ACV in as much water as you like. Over the coming days and weeks, gradually work up to having one tablespoon of ACV while you gradually decrease the amount of water. If you would prefer lemon juice, start with the juice of half a lemon diluted to your tastes with warm water and gradually work up to having the juice of a whole lemon in less warm water.

There is no better way to start the day than lemon in warm water and a *Real Food Chef* breakfast!

Food Combining

Food combining is a wonderful approach to eating that can enhance digestion, energy, vitality, and fat loss, and it can be a great way to combat a bloated tummy.

It involves a few simple principles including eating animal protein separate from starchy carbohydrates. In practice, that means no meat and potatoes on the same plate. It means that if you eat meat, chicken, or fish, you eat it with high-water vegetables and no starchy vegetables, such as potato, sweet potato, pumpkin, corn, or any other starchy foods such as pasta, bread, or rice. If you eat vegetable protein such as one of the many types of lentils, chickpeas, beans, or tempeh, then, under food-combining principles, you do not eat meat with these foods, but rather any vegetable at all, including starchy ones if they appeal. If you feel like eating rice, then, with food combining, it needs to be a vegetarian meal. Oils and other foods rich in fats including avocado can be eaten with either animal-based meals or starch-based meals.

Another principle of food combining is that fruit is only consumed as your first meal and not again during the day. You are also encouraged to omit all refined sugar due to its acidifying effects on the blood. I know people who live by the concept of food combining and feel spectacular. For others, for whom this seems extreme, but who still want to try it, I suggest they apply the zigzag principle. This means that most of the time they follow food-combining principles (zig), while one day a week or two to three meals a week they relax the principles and they zag. This way, it is a sustainable way to live as you are able to socialise and you can also eat the foods you might love but just not every day.

Remember it is what you do every day that impacts on your health, not what you do sometimes.

Food combining is a structured way of eating on which some people literally thrive, and I have truly seen this change people's lives. For some, it would take every aspect of joy out of their life. If this is the case, focusing on food combining is not for you right now or perhaps the zigzag concept might appeal.

Most of the meals in *Real Food Chef* follow food-combining principles.

Meat and Fish

THE FOCUS OF THIS COOKBOOK IS TO ENCOURAGE YOU TO INCREASE THE PLANT CONTENT OF YOUR DIET AS WELL AS THE NUTRIENT DENSITY. MANY PEOPLE WOULD ARGUE THAT MOST PEOPLE GENERALLY KNOW HOW TO COOK MEAT AND IT IS NOT OFTEN THIS AREA OF COOKING SKILLS THAT REQUIRES AN INJECTION OF CREATIVITY. HOWEVER, INCREASING THE APPEAL OF SILVER BEET FOR THE WHOLE FAMILY IS MORE LIKELY TO BE AN AREA WHERE WE NEED SOME HELP.

Nutrition polarises people. We all eat and therefore, we all have our own opinions about what constitutes a healthy diet. I always encourage people to eat in a way that nourishes their body, mind and soul and for some this means following a vegetarian or vegan diet. The base of the *Real Food Chef* recipes is vegan or vegetarian and they can be kept that way. Most of the dishes that do contain animal protein can also be altered back to their plant base. However, we also acknowledge that a lot of people choose to eat meat and/or fish and describe feeling more nourished when they include it in their diet.

THE *REAL FOOD CHEF* MESSAGE IS SIMPLE: EAT WHAT NOURISHES YOU AND USE THE RECIPES IN THE WAY THAT YOU WANT TO, WITH OR WITHOUT MEAT.

Most of the vegetarian meals mention an option to add fish, chicken, or lamb, if you want to feed an omnivorous family. We have included these meat options as recognition of their nutritive value. But at the heart of the *Real Food Chef* message is to encourage families to start focusing on increasing their consumption of plant food while still incorporating meat options, if different family members have differing needs and desires. Organic lamb, for example, provides protein, B-group vitamins including B1, B2, B3, B6 and B12, as well as the minerals, iron and zinc.

When it comes to choosing your meat we suggest you opt for grass-fed, free range or preferably organic. I am very aware of and appreciate these options may cost more economically. However, in my opinion and my observation of people's diets over the last 14 years, there are a lot of people who would benefit from reducing their portion sizes of meat. Choose good-quality cuts of meat and serve approximately a fist in size for a main meal.

When it comes to seafood we experience great divide again. Understandably there is reason for concern about including seafood in your diet, as more information is emerging about heavy metal contamination. Reducing your exposure to mercury is essential. The recipes we have included are typically made with small, white fish, which have a lower risk of mercury contamination. Small fish are a better choice because they have had less exposure and time to accumulate mercury.

Fish is an example of a nutrient-dense food. Besides containing protein and nutrients such as selenium and vitamin D, fish also contain the anti-inflammatory omega-3 fatty acids. Clinically, omega-3 fatty acids have been shown to reduce the risk of developing many degenerative diseases including heart disease. For pregnant women, breastfeeding mothers, and women of childbearing age, fish can supply the body with DHA, an omega-3 fatty acid that is beneficial for brain development. Flaxseeds (linseeds) are high in another omega-3 fatty acid known as EPA. The human body can convert EPA into DHA, a process that is upregulated during pregnancy. Again I encourage you to eat what nourishes you. Just be sure to include some omega-3-rich foods.

We have also included organic chicken in the book as it is often a family favorite. A good source of protein, chicken also contains niacin, which helps the body convert food into fuel. Niacin is also involved in the production of sex and stress hormones in the adrenal glands. It also contains methionine, an amino acid involved in mood regulation and the maintenance of our DNA.

If you eat chicken, purchasing organic chicken is highly recommended. Organically grown chickens have been fed an organically grown diet and have been raised without the use of antibiotics and free-range chickens are allowed access to the outdoors as opposed to being confined to the henhouse, with some producers also feeding them an organic diet.

If yours has been a "meat with every meal" household up until now, consider starting "meatless Mondays" and eat only plant-based foods that day. Once you and/or family members experience the taste sensation of a vegetable-based meal from the *Real Food Chef*, you may find three vegetarian meals per week become an easy option. Keep in mind, too, the recommendations from the most respected source of cancer prevention research and information, the World Cancer Research Fund (WCRF), who state: "Limit your intake of meat to no more than 300 grams per week and avoid processed meat." ○

Don't go meatless if it is not your thing. Just eat way more vegetables and other plant foods than meat.

Fats

NUTRITION INFORMATION TENDS TO MOVE IN CYCLES. WHETHER THE CURRENT FOCUS IS ON DECREASING CARBOHYDRATES OR INCREASING PROTEIN, ONE THING SEEMS TO REMAIN CONSTANT: MANY PEOPLE HAVE A FEAR OF FAT.

However, what is commonly misunderstood is the essential role fats play in our diet. Not all fat is created equal. Fats are composed of building blocks called fatty acids, just as proteins are comprised of their building blocks, amino acids.

There are three major categories of fatty acids: saturated, polyunsaturated, and monounsaturated. Of concern more recently is the generation of trans fats, found mainly in processed foods, specifically deep-fried foods, bought cakes, biscuits and muesli bars. Some research suggests that the type of fat you eat is actually more important than the total amount. Depending on the current state of your diet, I often encourage people to consume more fats, particularly from whole-food sources.

CONSUMING ADEQUATE FAT AND THE RIGHT FATS HELPS YOU TO MANAGE YOUR MOOD AND STAY ALERT, AND EVEN ASSISTS WITH WEIGHT MANAGEMENT.

Fats are also needed for helping us absorb vitamins such as A D, E, and K, as well as for maintaining healthy skin. They are an integral part of our immunity and brain development. Fat is also our most concentrated source of energy, and helps to keep us warm and protect our organs. The Mediterranean diet is high in monounsaturated fats, which are found in olive oil, avocados, nuts and seeds. The Mediterranean diet is linked with low blood pressure and lower incidences of heart disease.

By choosing *Real Food Chef* foods and meals you will naturally avoid poor-quality fats such as trans fats. If you experience sweet cravings in the afternoon, add more fat to your meals, particularly at lunch (and even more so if it was very low in fat), in the form of avocado, olive oil, avocado oil, nuts, organic butter, tahini or coconut oil and observe if your desire for sweet foods mid-afternoon diminishes. Many people have become scared of using oils and nuts due to their high energy content but good fats actually slow down the release of glucose into your bloodstream, requiring less insulin (a fat-storage hormone discussed at length in *Accidentally Overweight*), and meaning you actually stay full for longer.

In a nutshell...

Fats are a vital component of the human diet. There are numerous types of fats, some of which are essential for survival. This means that the body cannot synthesise them and that they must be eaten.

The different types of fats are:

- Saturated such as those found in coconut and organic butter
- Monounsaturated such as those found in olives, avocadoes, and macadamia nuts, and oils made from these foods
- Polyunsaturated fats of which there are two types:
  - Omega-6 such as those found predominantly in nuts and seeds and oils made from these foods
  - Omega-3 such as those found in oily fish, linseeds (flaxseeds), walnuts and pecans

The fats above all have crucial roles to play in obtaining and maintaining optimal health. They help our immune system defend us from infection, they help create our sex hormones and they help mediate inflammation... the list is almost endless.

You have to eat fat to burn fat and I've met thousands of people who eat too little. If you eliminate it or eat too small an amount, your body tends to believe that there is some sort of famine going on and it stores body fat thinking it is doing you a big favour, helping you get through this period of supposed restriction.

The fats included in the *Real Food Chef* meals are from whole-food sources. They add to the satiety factor of each meal as well as the nutritional content. For the body to be able to extract fat-soluble vitamins from food, for example, it must be in the presence of fat. I am asked so often, "How much avocado can I eat?" and what I know is that when you start to eat the *Real Food Chef* way, you will be able to answer your own question.

Your body is your best guide and I want you in touch with its signals rather than having them masked by a diet full of processed fats, and refined sugars and flours. There will be days when half an avocado will serve you at lunchtime while on other days, only a whole one will do. You might begin to notice that when it is in the presence of lemon juice and herbs it tastes even better and taste may be one of the aspects you need in your food for it to be satisfying.

Choose fat from real food sources. Your skin, your hair and your eyes (just to name a few) will love you for it ○.

IT IS WHAT YOU DO EVERY DAY THAT IMPACTS ON YOUR HEALTH, NOT WHAT YOU DO SOMETIMES.

— DR LIBBY

Berry Quinoa Porridge (p.53)

Breakfast

Essene Bread with Poached Egg and Greens (p.45))

Pumpkin Pancakes with Maple Pecans and Coconut yoghurt (p.61)

Breakfast Salad (p.55)

Hash Brown Potatoes (p.63)

Breakfast

Other than beginning the day with gratitude for our gift of life, some breath-focused movement and a glass of warm water with lemon juice, a nutrient-dense breakfast is key to a happy and energetic start to the day. Without breakfast, our blood glucose tends to fall, which can leave us gritty and fatigued, and experiencing a lousy frame of mind and mood to begin a brand new day.

From a nutritional and a biochemical perspective, it is literally time to break your fast. Having most likely not eaten for 12 hours or so, your body is in need of nutrients and fuel so it is able to give you a feeling of energy, create the neurotransmitters necessary for happiness, power your immune system to keep you well, as well as supporting thousands of other vital functions that literally keep you alive. Pause and think about that. The body is truly a spectacular creation.

Not only does your blood glucose need stabilising through appropriate nourishment at this time, but what you choose to eat and drink at breakfast either sets you up for smooth sailing or big challenges when it comes to your food choices, energy and your mood later in the day.

The beginning of the day can be the perfect time to enjoy fruit, best eaten on an empty stomach. If you suffer with digestive-system problems such as diarrhoea or bloating, it would be wise to make this the only fruit of the day (or omit it entirely if you have known fructose malabsorption).

I am a huge fan of incorporating fruit and vegetables into a smoothie at this time of day and you'll find a selection of them in our Smoothies & Drinks section. A green smoothie, for example, is a brilliant way to start the day as it ticks all of my boxes when it comes to the outcomes I want for you and your body: it supports optimal blood pH due to the green vegetable content; it supports liver detoxification pathways as well as your energy systems. You may also like to follow this with one of the delicious, nutrient-dense breakfast options included in this section.

I am also a fan of challenging the concept of what many consider to be a conventional breakfast. Any of the meals in this book are suitable for any time of the day. So for variety, if that appeals to you, feel free to choose something from the lunch section to enjoy for breakfast. I want to encourage you to truly listen to what your body needs and make a selection based on nourishing your own body, rather than from a prescribed list of permitted foods or meals. For example, you may feel cold and therefore prefer a warming meal at particular times of the year or even all year round. Your body doesn't have a voice but it will always let you know whether it is happy or not. It is up to us to decipher its whispers, growls and smiles and to notice the energy and clarity of mind (or not) on offer.

All of the *Real Food Chef* meals are designed to set you up for a day of even and outstanding energy and they pack an almighty nutrient punch. Look out brand new day... here you come!

Egg Crepe

Egg Crepe

Ingredients

Crepes

1 big bunch spinach, cleaned

¼ cup peas (fresh or frozen)

salt and ground black pepper

3 large eggs

¼ cup almond milk or filtered water

avocado oil or coconut oil for sautéing

¼ cup flat-leaf parsley, finely chopped

Salsa

1 tomato, finely diced

1 avocado, peeled and finely diced

pinch of cumin

salt and ground black pepper

1 tablespoon spring onion, chopped

¼ cup fresh coriander, chopped

Method

Crepes:

1. Lightly steam or sauté the spinach and drain.
2. Add the peas to the same pan as the spinach and gently cook. Remove from the heat and season with the salt and pepper.
3. Whisk together the eggs and almond milk or water. Heat the oil in a medium skillet and pour in the eggs.
4. As the eggs begin to set, sprinkle them with the chopped parsley. Place the spinach and peas in the middle. When the bottom of the eggs is lightly browned, gently roll the egg over into a roll. Serve with salsa or Red Sauce (page 227).

Salsa:

1. Gently mix the chopped tomato and avocado.
2. Season the mixture with the ground cumin, and a little salt and pepper if desired.

Serves 1-2 | 15 minutes

Nutritional Information

This crepe is perfect for a light brunch or breakfast. It's filled with greens and contains protein, folate and vitamin E. Enjoy the alkalising effect of the spinach and peas while savouring the rich and filling flavours of this simple dish.

Essene Bread with Poached Egg and Greens

Essene Bread with Poached Egg and Greens

Ingredients

Eggs:

2 large eggs

2 tablespoons apple cider vinegar

200g fresh spinach, cleaned

2 large asparagus stalks

1 slice Essene bread

salt and ground black pepper

Essential Seed Mix:

¼ cup sunflower seeds

¼ cup pumpkin seeds

¼ cup black sesame seeds

¼ cup white sesame seeds

Serves 1-2 | 15 minutes

Method

1. Poach the eggs in a large pan of boiling water with 2 tablespoons of vinegar added. Remove the finished eggs with a slotted spoon.
2. In another pan, bring a small amount of salted water to a boil and blanch the asparagus stalks. Remove them and refresh under cold running water when they are just tender, about 2 minutes.
3. Immerse the spinach in the same pan of boiling water as the asparagus. When it has just wilted, remove it and drain on a tea towel. Season with salt and pepper.

To assemble:

1. Cut a 2cm slice of the Essene bread. Arrange the spinach and asparagus on the bread. Top with the poached eggs.
2. Sprinkle the essential seed mix over the top of the eggs and greens and store the remainder of the seed mix in an airtight container.

Note

This recipe is easily split for 2 servings. Add a green salad with Udo's oil and balsamic dressing, or more simply steamed vegetables, for a complete meal, ideal for a light brunch.

Nutritional Information

Plant-based diets have been shown to be especially effective in the prevention of numerous chronic diseases, including diabetes, heart disease and some cancers. Start your day in the same manner as many healthy populations: with lots of vegetables. The seed mix boosts the nutritional profile even further by adding zinc, magnesium and dietary fibre.

The Real Food Chef Muesli

The Real Food Chef Muesli

Ingredients

¼ cup whole millet

¼ cup whole amaranth

¼ cup whole buckwheat groats

¼ cup whole linseeds

¼ cup sesame seeds

¼ cup pumpkin seeds

¼ cup sunflower seeds

¼ cup currants

Makes 2 cups | 5 minutes

Method

1. Mix all the ingredients until well blended. Store in a glass or plastic container with a tight-fitting lid.

Nutritional Information:

It's hard to name a nutrient not found in this recipe. Not many types of muesli on the market are based on seeds, but they are a nutritional powerhouse, packed in particular with beneficial minerals, including calcium, magnesium and zinc. Using currants means you will have fruit that does not contain preservatives, while still getting a hint of sweetness.

The Real Food Chef Bircher Muesli

The Real Food Chef Bircher Muesli

Ingredients

Muesli:

¼ cup whole millet

¼ cup whole amaranth

¼ cup whole buckwheat groats

¼ cup whole linseeds

¼ cup sesame seeds

¼ cup pumpkin seeds

¼ cup sunflower seeds

¼ cup currants

Coconut Yoghurt:

flesh of 1 young coconut

1 teaspoon maple syrup

⅓ cup coconut water

½ cup raw cashew nuts

pinch of salt

Serves 3-4 | 15 minutes + overnight

Method

Muesli:

1. Mix all dry muesli ingredients until evenly distributed. Add ½ cup of coconut water and coconut yoghurt to your liking to form Bircher muesli. Can be left to soak overnight.

Coconut Yoghurt:

1. Open the young coconut and drain the coconut water into a bowl or jug. Scoop the flesh of the coconut using a spoon. Blend the coconut flesh with the maple syrup, coconut water, cashew nuts and salt in a blender until smooth.

Nutritional Information:

This muesli mix is packed full of minerals. It is a good source of magnesium, essential for bones, muscle function and relaxation processes. Millet contains tryptophan, an amino acid precursor to serotonin, our happy hormone. This muesli is also high in fibre, essential for outstanding elimination.

Coconut Yoghurt

Ingredients

Muesli:

flesh of 1 young coconut

⅓ cup coconut water

½ cup raw cashew nuts

1 teaspoon maple syrup

pinch of salt

Makes 1½ cups | 20 minutes

Method

1. Open the young coconut and drain the water into a bowl or jug, measure out ⅓ cup and reserve the rest.
2. Scoop the flesh out of the coconut using a spoon.
3. Combine the coconut flesh and water with the cashews, maple syrup and salt to taste. Blend in a blender until the mixture is smooth.

Tip

Use the rest of the coconut water for our smoothies.

Serve with fresh fruit, summer berries, baked pears or the *Real Food Chef* Muesli.

Nutritional Information:

This yoghurt is perfect for those looking for a dairy-free alternative to regular yoghurt, but who still want good flavour, texture and beneficial vitamins and minerals. The fats of the coconut and cashews slow the release of gastric emptying of the stomach, allowing you to feel fuller longer and evening out blood-glucose levels.

Berry Quinoa Porridge

Berry Quinoa Porridge

Ingredients

Berry and Almond Mixture:

2 Medjool dates, pitted and coarsely chopped

1 cup raw almonds, soaked overnight, then rinsed well

3 cups filtered water

1 cup blueberries (fresh or frozen)

pinch of salt

Quinoa:

1 cup tri-colour quinoa

2 cups filtered water

pinch of ground cinnamon

Serves 3-4 | 25 minutes

Method

Berry Mixture:

1. Combine all the berry mixture ingredients in a blender and blend until smooth.

Quinoa:

1. Bring the 2 cups of water to a boil with the pinch of cinnamon. Stir in the quinoa, stir once or twice, then lower the heat and cover the pan.
2. Cook the quinoa until it has thickened and absorbed all the water.
3. Serve the quinoa in a bowl and pour the berry and almond mixture over it.

Note

You can serve the porridge warm or cold, with warm or cold berry sauce. To make an even more substantial meal, serve it with baked pears, shredded coconut and a sprinkling of the essential seed mix.

Nutritional Information:

This is a wonderful gluten-free alternative to regular porridge. It is packed with vitamin E, protein and fibre, keeping you fuller for longer. Even though it is a hearty porridge, it is gentle and warming on sensitive digestive systems.

Breakfast Salad on Essene Bread

Breakfast Salad on Essene Bread

Ingredients

2 large eggs
1 tablespoon apple cider vinegar
1 slice Essene bread
4 cherry tomatoes, halved
1 small cucumber, chopped
¼ cup red capsicum, seeded and chopped
¼ cup yellow capsicum, seeded and chopped
1 cup spinach leaves
¼ cup fresh basil, julienned

Serves 1-2 | 20 minutes

Method

1. Bring a medium pot of water to boil and add the vinegar.
2. Poach the eggs for about 3 to 5 minutes. Remove with a slotted spoon.
3. Tear up the Essene bread into large chunks and toss with the vegetables and herbs.
4. Dress the salad with a dressing of your choice — try a maple and balsamic vinegar dressing with this salad.
5. Top the tossed salad with the poached eggs and garnish with living sprouts or essential seeds, if desired.

Nutritional Information:

Having a salad for breakfast is a great way of increasing the nutrient content of your diet and boosting alkalinity. For those of you who need to avoid gluten, just substitute a piece of gluten-free bread of your choice. Don't forget this fresh and cooling salad for a warm-weather brunch or light lunch.

HERBED SCRAMBLED EGG

Herbed Scrambled Egg

Ingredients

2 large eggs

¼ cup fresh parsley, chopped

1 teaspoon coconut oil

1 cup spinach leaves

1 slice of Essene bread

1 wedge of lemon

pumpkin seeds to serve

Serves 1 | 10 minutes

Method

1. Add the coconut oil to a pan over a medium heat.
2. In a small bowl gently whisk eggs and chopped parsley.
3. Add egg mixture to frying pan and move around for approximately 1–2 minutes.
4. Serve on top of raw spinach and a slice of Essene bread, with freshly squeezed lemon juice and pumpkin seeds.

Nutritional Information:

This dish is the perfect quick breakfast and a superior alternative to a processed breakfast cereal. Fresh parsley is an excellent source of vitamins C and K and is highly alkaline. Parsley is my favorite food!

Breakfast Hash with Mushrooms

Breakfast Hash with Mushrooms

Ingredients

4 large eggs

¼ cup filtered water

1 teaspoon coconut oil

¼ cup leek, sliced

1 cup button mushrooms, chopped

salt and ground black pepper

2 leaves silver beet
or 2 cups of baby spinach or kale

1 tomato, chopped or ¼ cup cherry tomatoes, halved

¼ cup peas (fresh or frozen)

1 ¼ cups parsley, chopped

Serves 2 | 20 minutes

Method

1. In a bowl, gently whisk eggs and water until combined.
2. On high heat with coconut oil, cook leek and mushroom, and season with salt and pepper.
3. Turn the heat down, and add silver beet, tomato, peas, and parsley. Sauté to allow flavors to combine and moisture to be released from mushroom and tomato.
4. Pour egg into the pan and allow to cook, folding it through gently with a wooden spoon to prevent burning. Cook for approximately 2 minutes or until egg has just set.

Tip

Serve on top of a slice of Essene or good quality bread and a good handful of flat-leaf parsley.

Nutritional Information:

Essene bread has a nutty and surprisingly sweet flavor. Made from sprouted wheat, it is gentler on the digestive system than ordinary wheat and much more nutrient-dense. Essene bread contains no yeast, sweeteners, flour, oil or preservatives. Eggs are high in protein. This is a great breakfast for a big day!

Pumpkin Pancakes with Maple Pecans and Coconut Yoghurt

Pumpkin Pancakes with Maple Pecans and Coconut Yoghurt

Ingredients

1 cup pumpkin, cooked and mashed

pinch of turmeric

1 ¾ cups almond milk or filtered water

¼ cup maple syrup

2 large eggs

1 ½ cups quinoa flour

2 teaspoons baking powder

½ teaspoon ground cinnamon

½ teaspoon ground ginger

½ teaspoon salt

2 tablespoons coconut oil

To Serve:

3 tablespoons maple syrup

½ cup raw pecans

3 tablespoons coconut yoghurt

Method

1. Cut and peel a medium-size pumpkin and chop it roughly. Put it in a large saucepan with water to cover. Add the turmeric and cook until soft.
2. Drain the pieces of pumpkin. Mash the pumpkin and measure out enough for 1 cup.
3. Add the pumpkin, almond milk or water, maple syrup, eggs, quinoa flour, baking powder, cinnamon, ginger and salt into a blender and blend until smooth.

To Cook:

1. Grease a skillet or griddle with a tablespoon of the coconut oil over medium heat.
2. Pour ¼ cup portions of the batter into the skillet, two at a time. Flip them over when bubbles begin to rise to the surface of the pancake and the underside is golden brown. Cook for 20 to 30 seconds on the second side, or until the centre springs back when pressed.
3. Continue in this manner until all the batter has been used.
4. Serve a stack of pancakes for each person. Put a portion of the pecans in the centre of the top pancake and spoon some of the maple syrup over them. Top with a dollop of the coconut yoghurt.

Makes 8-10 | 25 minutes

Nutritional Information:

Using the quinoa flour is a better health alternative to regular all-purpose flour, as the quinoa includes amino acids crucial to the synthesis of proteins and liver detoxification. The pumpkin provides moisture and beta-carotene. Adding ground cinnamon and ginger adds a warming component good for digestion and blood-glucose regulation.

Hashbrown Potatoes

Hashbrown Potatoes

Ingredients

2 medium or 3 small agria or cream delight potatoes, washed and grated

½ medium sweet potato, peeled and grated

4 to 6 tablespoons spelt flour

1 spring onion, roughly chopped

salt and black ground pepper

2 tablespoons coconut or macadamia oil for frying

Serves 3-4 | 25 minutes

Method

1. Mix the grated potatoes and sweet potato. Stir in the flour and chopped spring onion. Season with the salt and pepper.
2. Squeeze the mixture in your hands to release as much of the starch as possible.
3. Heat the oil in a small skillet over medium heat. Make a mound of ¼ cup potato mixture, then gently press it down into a circle.
4. Cook the potatoes until golden brown on each side, about 3 to 5 minutes. Add extra oil in between times if needed.

Tip

Gluten-free flour can be substituted for the spelt flour.

Nutritional Information:

The addition of the sweet potato lowers the glycemic load of this delicious dish, meaning you will feel fuller for longer. A healthy alternative to the processed, packaged version, we've used organic vegetables as they add a natural sweetness to these hashbrowns.

Roasted Vegetable Frittata Muffins with Red Sauce

Roasted Vegetable Frittata Muffins with Red Sauce

Ingredients

Muffins:

6 large eggs

1 cup almond milk or filtered water

3 cups assorted roasted vegetables (pumpkin, mushroom, capsicum and zucchini)

1 cup quinoa, cooked, half white and half black

1 cup fresh basil leaves, julienned

¼ cup parsley, chopped

salt and ground black pepper

Red Sauce:

1 cup raw cashew nuts

⅓ cup olive oil

1 red capsicum, seeded and chopped

1 tablespoon fresh red chili, seeded and finely chopped

juice of ½ lemon

2 Medjool dates, pitted and coarsely chopped

Serves 6 | 35 minutes

Method

Muffins:

1. Preheat the oven to 170°C.
2. Whisk together the eggs and milk.
3. Combine the roasted vegetables and quinoa with the basil and parsley. Pour the milk mixture into the vegetables and season with salt and pepper.
4. Stir the mixture until it is well blended. Pour the mixture into muffin pans and bake in the hot oven for about 30 minutes.
5. Serve with red sauce drizzled over.

Red Sauce:

1. Combine all the ingredients and blend until smooth.

Nutritional Information:

Start your day off with these nutrient-packed muffins. High in protein, they are also suitable as a snack or for lunch. Add a salad or loads of greens to amp up the alkalinity.

Every time you spend money,
you are casting a vote
for the kind of world you want.
— Dr Libby

Chocolate Pumpkin Seed Skin Shake (p.83)

Smoothies

Pina Colada (p.91)

Almond Date Shake (p.85)

Green Smoothie (p.75)

Banana Berry and Coconut Smoothie (p.77)

Smoothies and Drinks

Smoothies truly can't get more nourishing and delicious than these options. Perfect snacks or nutrient boosts, these drinks have the right balance of minerals and water to keep you hydrated and fueled.

The popularity of smoothies and juices continues to grow. We just want to make sure the ones you choose are made with quality ingredients. Bought juices and smoothies, in some instances, have more sugar than their soft-drink counterparts. The philosophy of the *Real Food Chef* means keeping sugar quantities from all sources (from fruit or pure maple syrup in the RFC way) lower than the vegetable content.

Fruits are highly nutritious and if you digest them well, then it is an excellent choice. However, with fructose as the source of carbohydrate in fruit often not being well tolerated by people who suffer with irritable bowel, flatulence and gas, it suits some people to reduce or, for a period, omit fruit. For some people fruit serves them if eaten on an empty stomach in the morning. If you know your body tolerates fruit well I still want you to consider the amount you consume. It is my belief that the guidelines around fruit consumption have been misinterpreted by many people. When it comes to fruit, two pieces a day is ideal and using berries is a great low-fructose choice.

In today's busy world it can be difficult to find the time to sit down to the amount of plant foods we are suggesting. Green smoothies and drinks containing fruit and vegetables are a very easy way of increasing the nutrient-density of your diet. I will often make the green smoothie recipe and keep it in a drink bottle to drink for morning tea. This smoothie recipe can be progressed into a blueberry and chocolate smoothie. The blueberry and chocolate smoothie variations will appeal to most children as well. A smoothie can be a wonderful way to start your day or a great snack any time of the day!

Almond Milk

ALMOND MILK

INGREDIENTS

1 cup raw almonds, soaked overnight, then rinsed well

pinch sea salt

¼ teaspoon vanilla extract

3 cups filtered water

METHOD

1. Combine the soaked almonds with the salt and vanilla in a blender. Process the mixture until it is coarsely chopped.
2. Pour in the water with the motor running and process until the ingredients are very well ground.
3. Strain the mixture through a piece of hessian cloth and collect it in a bowl or jar. Milk is strained to get the right consistency. Add back the almond meal if you don't mind a more coarse texture.
4. Use the almond milk as you would any other milk, keeping it refrigerated until ready to use.

Makes 3 cups | 10 minutes

NUTRITIONAL INFORMATION:

Almond milk is a nutrient-dense alternative to both cow's milk and non-dairy milk alternatives. Besides its delicious, nutty flavor, almond milk contains beneficial amounts of vitamin E and calcium.

Green Smoothie

Green Smoothie

Ingredients

water from a large, young coconut, about 1 cup

150g fresh spinach leaves or silver beet leaves

1 to 2 bananas, peeled, chopped and frozen

Method

1. Drain the water from the coconut. Set aside.
2. Remove the stem and coarsely chop the silver beet if using.
3. Combine all ingredients and blend until smooth. Add more water if you prefer a thinner smoothie.

Serves 1-2 | 10 minutes

Note

The silver beet will make a darker smoothie than the spinach. You may wish to add an extra banana for sweetness until you get used to a green smoothie.

Nutritional Information:

Start the day with a green smoothie to increase your leafy green vegetable consumption. A diet high in plants has been shown to decrease the risk of developing degenerative diseases including type 2 diabetes, heart disease and some cancers. Wow! Such a simple way to “amp up your greens”.

Blueberry Green Smoothie

Blueberry Green Smoothie

Ingredients

150g fresh spinach

water from a large, young coconut, about 1 cup

1 medium banana, peeled, chopped and frozen

1 ½ cups blueberries (fresh or frozen)

Serves 1-2 | 10 minutes

Method

1. Combine all ingredients and blend until smooth.

Nutritional Information:

This nutrient-charged drink contains super amounts of dietary fibre, vitamins, minerals and chlorophyll. The blueberries add beneficial antioxidants to up the anti-aging power of this quick and easy drink. The electrolytes in the coconut water make it great for hydration as well.

Chocolate Think Shake

CHOCOLATE THINK SHAKE

INGREDIENTS

150g fresh spinach

water from a large, young coconut, about 1 cup

1 medium banana, peeled, chopped and frozen

1 cup of blueberries (fresh or frozen)

½ cup cacao powder

¼ cup maple syrup

Serves 1-2 | 10 minutes

METHOD

1. Combine all ingredients and blend until smooth.

NUTRITIONAL INFORMATION:

It might be hard to believe that there is a substantial amount of fresh spinach in this thick and creamy shake. Increase your nutrient-density simply with this quick and tasty beverage. Along with the hydrating benefits of coconut water, this delicious shake delivers vital amounts of potassium, folate and magnesium as well as packing a huge antioxidant punch!

Pumpkin Seed Milk Shake

Pumpkin Seed Milk Shake

Ingredients

1 cup pumpkin seeds

1 medium banana, peeled, chopped and frozen

4 Medjool dates, pitted and coarsely chopped

¼ large avocado, or ½ small avocado

¼ teaspoon pure vanilla extract

pinch of salt

3 to 4 cups filtered water

Serves 1-2 | 10 minutes

Method

1. Combine all ingredients and blend until smooth.

Nutritional Information:

This is the perfect shake for anyone with skin problems. The nutrients in the banana, pumpkin seeds and avocado are highly beneficial for troubled complexions. Have a shake as a snack and give yourself a healthy dose of zinc in the process.

Chocolate Pumpkin Seed Skin Shake

Chocolate Pumpkin Seed Skin Shake

Ingredients

1 cup pumpkin seeds

1 medium banana, peeled, chopped and frozen

4 Medjool dates, pitted and coarsely chopped

¼ cup cacao powder

½ small or ¼ large avocado

¼ teaspoon pure vanilla essence

3 cups filtered water

pinch of salt

Serves 1-2 | 10 minutes

Method

1. Combine all ingredients and blend until smooth.

Nutritional Information:

A great breakfast or filling snack due to the satiating addition of avocado. Nicknamed the "Skin Shake" due to the high content of zinc and monounsaturated fats, it will have you glowing in no time. Cacao powder is the rawest form of chocolate and is very high in antioxidants. It does contain caffeine so it is best consumed in the morning. We like to follow this drink with a lovely big glass of water.

Almond Date Shake

ALMOND DATE SHAKE

INGREDIENTS

2 cups almond milk

2 large bananas, peeled, chopped and frozen

2 to 3 Medjool dates, pitted and coarsely chopped

dash of vanilla or cinnamon

Serves 1-2 | 10 minutes

METHOD

1. Combine all ingredients and blend until smooth.

NUTRITIONAL INFORMATION:

Essentially a vitamin E shake, this antioxidant-rich drink is a great way to start the day, or consume it as a snack before or after exercise. It is also rich in potassium thanks to the bananas, and dates contain iron and a host of other minerals.

Banana, Berry and Coco[illegible]oothie

Banana, Berry and Coconut Smoothie

Ingredients

1 medium banana, peeled, chopped and frozen

1 cup blueberries (fresh or frozen)

water from 1 large, young coconut, about 1 cup

Method

1. Combine all ingredients and blend until smooth.

Serves 1 | 10 minutes

Nutritional Information:

This smoothie is more than just a delicious thirst quencher. The isotonic nature of the coconut water means it has beneficial hydrating values. Try this quick and easy smoothie anytime of the day or after a workout. It speeds recovery due to its electrolyte and antioxidant content.

Mint and Lime Berry Mocktai

Mint and Lime Berry Mocktail

Ingredients

½ lime

½ cup fresh mint

1 medium banana, peeled, chopped and frozen

1 cup blueberries (fresh or frozen)

water from a large, young coconut, about 1 cup

pinch of salt

Serves 1-2 | 5 minutes

Method

1. Remove the skin from the lime.
2. Chop the lime into small pieces and place in blender.
3. Add all remaining ingredients and blend until smooth.

Nutritional Information:

This pretty drink is a delicious thirst quencher. The isotonic nature of coconut water means it is particularly hydrating. With the addition of lime, this zesty mocktail is a liver-friendly, health-enhancing alternative to a cocktail.

Pina Colada Mocktail

PINA COLADA MOCKTAIL

INGREDIENTS

1 medium pineapple, peeled, cored and cut into chunks, about 2 cups

water from a large, young coconut, about 1 cup

juice of ½ lime, optional

METHOD

1. Lay the pineapple chunks on a small tray lined with waxed paper and freeze them.
2. Crack open the coconut and drain the water.
3. Combine all ingredients and blend until smooth.

Serves 1-2 | 10 minutes

NUTRITIONAL INFORMATION:

An alcohol-free cocktail with simple and fresh ingredients. The water from a young coconut is particularly hydrating, a good thing to know on a hot afternoon. Pineapple is an excellent source of manganese and vitamin C. The enzyme bromelain is a natural digestive for protein and is found in abundance in fresh pineapple. Happiness in a glass.

It is more fun to talk with someone
who doesn't use long,
difficult words but rather short,
easy words like "What's for lunch?"

— Winnie the Pooh

Pesto Noodle Salad with Chicken (p.105)

Lunch

Thai Pumpkin Soup (p.103)

Quinoa Fried Rice (p.111)

Quinoa Sushi (p.117)

Green Lentil Tabouli with White Fish (p.113)

Lunch

If you are supporting yourself with the right breakfast you have already set your day up for smooth sailing. Lunch is a crucial point in your day where you can stop, gather your thoughts and refuel — however, how many of us consider our lunch in this way?

Engulfing anything you see in your path at 4pm is not what I consider a nourishing lunch. Preparing your own food and having it with you not only saves you money, it also ensures your lunch is a nutrient-dense and energising meal. You are not doing anyone, especially yourself, any favours by skipping lunch, so set yourself a reminder and stop. Consider this — you've already been busy all morning and you're possibly about to do it again all afternoon. By taking those few moments to breathe and eat slowly, you will enter the afternoon feeling refreshed and invigorated.

The philosophy of the *Real Food Chef* is about increasing the nutrition of your diet mainly through increasing your consumption of vegetables. In every meal I want you to consider how you might increase the nourishment of the meal. Protein is an important component of an energising lunch as it will help stabilise your blood glucose and offer a slow and even release of energy, particularly when paired with plenty of greens. Fat is also a vital part of every meal and most people find lunch far more satiating with a whole-food fat source included. This also tends to lead people to naturally choose a nourishing afternoon tea, rather than a quick fix devoid of nutrients.

The *Real Food Chef* lunch options have a few old favourites that have been transformed to meet the *Real Food Chef* seal of approval. Sushi is now a low-GI lunch with the inclusion of quinoa and the humble open sandwich has had greens and a beautiful sprouted bread added to ensure you are fueled into the afternoon. Food is designed to fuel you but for so many of us this is not the case. If your lunch leaves you feeling lethargic and sleepy it is time to revise your lunch choices.

A key component of the *Real Food Chef* way of eating is determining what works for you. During the cooler months you may want to focus on the warming options. You may notice these serve you better all year round. The climate of your home town may also influence this. Soups can be a beautiful option for lunch as you can pack them full of vegetables or you may choose to use recipes from breakfast or dinner at this time of the day.

Greenleaf Salad Wrap with Raw Hummus and Sprout Salad

Greenleaf Salad Wrap with Raw Hummus and Sprout Salad

Ingredients

4 large cos lettuce leaves
8 tablespoons raw hummus
1 cup baby spinach
1 cup live sprouts, such as broccoli or alfalfa
1 small carrot, peeled and grated
1 small beetroot, peeled and grated
1 large ripe tomato, thinly sliced
1 avocado, sliced
salt and ground black pepper
cooked skinless chicken breast, optional

Serves 1-2 | 15 minutes

Method

1. Remove 4 large lettuce leaves and remove the tough stem of each leaf. Put 2 leaves on each plate, placed on top of each other so the stem ends are on opposite sides.
2. Spread half the hummus down the centre of each set of leaves. Arrange the baby spinach on top of the hummus.
3. Layer the sprouts, carrot and beetroot over the hummus on each set of leaves, then top with the sliced tomato and avocado and season with salt and pepper.
4. Add the sliced chicken breast at this point if you are going to use it.
5. Roll the wraps, starting at one of the stem ends and rolling the wrap up lengthwise.

Nutritional Information:

Who needs bread when you can have your sandwich wrapped in nutrient-dense cos lettuce leaves? One of the real powerhouses of nutrition is the live sprouts, an excellent source of minerals, amino acids and phytochemicals. Add living sprouts to as many meals as you can.

Split Pea Soup

SPLIT PEA SOUP

INGREDIENTS

2 cups green split peas
1 bay leaf, crushed
3 curry leaves, crushed
2 litres filtered water
2 stalks celery, finely diced
1 large carrot, peeled and finely diced
1 small onion, finely diced
1 small clove garlic, minced
1 teaspoon ground cumin
salt and ground black pepper

TIP

Ladle a portion of the soup into a warmed, shallow bowl and centre a braised lamb shank on top of each one. You can also serve the thickened soup under a filet of fish seasoned with Indian spices, such as garam masala and cumin.

Serves 4-6 | 45 minutes

METHOD

1. Rinse the split peas under running water, then put them in a large saucepan with the crushed bay leaf, curry leaves and water. Bring the pot to a boil, then lower the heat. Skim off any impurities as they come to the surface and let the split peas simmer.
2. When the peas are tender to the bite, add the celery, carrot, onion and garlic. Simmer until the vegetables are cooked, adding more water if needed.
3. Season the soup with ground cumin, salt and pepper and simmer until the split peas are soft.

NUTRITIONAL INFORMATION:

Soothing for the digestive system, this soup is ideal for people who battle fatigue. The soup is packed with minerals and is nutrient-dense on its own. It can also form the nutritional base to a meal that may contain greens and/or animal protein.

THAI PUMPKIN SOUP

Thai Pumpkin Soup

Ingredients

½ pumpkin or butternut squash, peeled and cubed

1 large sweet potato, peeled and cubed

1 medium onion, chopped

2 tablespoons coconut oil

1 stalk lemongrass, white part only

5 leaves kaffir lime leaves, rubbed between your hands to release the oil

2 teaspoons curry powder

Salt and ground black pepper

3 slices galangal — substitute with fresh ginger if galangal is not available

1 small red chili, seeded and finely chopped

1 small bunch fresh parsley, finely chopped

½ tablespoon ground cumin

½ tablespoon ground coriander

1 ½ cups chicken or vegetable stock

3 ½ cups filtered water

1 can coconut milk

Method

1. Preheat the oven to 180°C.
2. Toss the pumpkin, sweet potato and onion with half the coconut oil and season with salt and pepper. Layer them on a baking sheet or roasting dish and bake for 20 to 30 minutes, or until they are caramelised. Stir them once or twice to prevent sticking.
3. With the reamining coconut oil sauté lemongrass, lime leaves and curry powder in a large saucepan.
4. Add the roasted vegetables and all remianing ingredients to the sautéed spices, except for the coconut milk.
5. Bring the pot to a simmer and cook for about 20 minutes over low heat. Add the coconut milk and gently heat it through.
6. Allow the soup to cool, then remove the lemongrass. Ladle the soup into a blender and process until smooth, working in batches if necessary. You can strain the soup through a fine mesh sieve if you prefer a creamier texture.

Serves 4-6 | 60 minutes | Freezer-friendly

Nutritional Information:

This fragrant and lightly spicy soup is perfect for those with poor circulation. Coconuts contain a beneficial saturated fat which is crucial to the anti-tumour response of the immune system. This soup is also rich in beta-carotene, vital for vision and healthy skin.

Pesto Noodle Salad with Chicken

Pesto Noodle Salad with Chicken

Ingredients

Chicken:

500g boneless skinless chicken breast

salt and ground black pepper

1 tablespoon macadamia nut oil

¼ cup fresh parsley, finely chopped

¼ cup fresh coriander, finely chopped

1 tablespoon red chili, seeded and finely chopped

Macadamia Pesto:

2 large cups basil leaves

1 cup raw macadamia nuts

juice of 1 lemon

salt and ground black pepper

½ to 1 cup filtered water

Salad:

1 cup pumpkin, peeled and cubed

1 tablespoon olive oil

pinch cinnamon

110g kelp noodles

5 to 6 cherry tomatoes, halved

2 tablespoons sprouted lentils (or sprouts of your choice)

½ medium red capsicum, seeded and thinly sliced

1 cup snow peas

Method

Chicken:

1. Preheat the oven to 180°C.
2. Season the chicken breast with the salt, pepper and oil. Coat it on both sides with the parsley, coriander and red chili.
3. Sear the prepared chicken in an oven-proof skillet for 1 minute on each side. Put the skillet in the hot oven and bake for 8 to 9 minutes, until it is completely cooked through. Let it rest while preparing the rest of the recipe.

Macadamia pesto:

1. Combine the macadamia nuts with the basil leaves in the bowl of a food processor or blender. Process until the nuts are well ground and the basil is well incorporated.
2. Add the lemon juice and season with salt and pepper. With the motor running, pour in the water. The pesto can be smooth or chunky.

Salad:

1. Toss the cubed pumpkin with the olive oil and cinnamon. Layer it in a baking dish and bake in the same oven as the chicken (180°C) until tender.
2. Once the chicken has rested, slice it against the grain.
3. Rinse the kelp noodles in cold water and combine with the roasted pumpkin, cherry tomatoes, sprouts, red capsicum and snow peas.
4. Toss the salad ingredients with the macadamia pesto, coating the mixture well.
5. Serve the salad with the sliced chicken on top, or cut the slices smaller and toss the chicken with the rest of the salad ingredients.

Serves 3-4 | 45 minutes

Nutritional Information:

Organic chicken is a good source of the essential amino acid methionine, important for vital neurotransmitter function and a healthy nervous system. Kelp noodles are a good source of iodine and a nutrient-dense alternative to wheat and egg noodles or pasta. Kelp noodles are vegan and gluten-free.

Quinoa and Roasted Vegetable Patty

Quinoa and Roasted Vegetable Patty

Ingredients

Roasted vegetables:

1 cup pumpkin, peeled and cubed

1 cup sweet potato, peeled and cubed

1 large onion, diced

1 large red capsicum, seeded and diced

1 medium zucchini, diced

1 cup button mushrooms, stemmed and quartered

1 small eggplant, cubed

2 tablespoons olive oil

salt and ground black pepper

1 sprig of rosemary, finely chopped

4 sprigs of thyme, leaves removed

1 bunch of fresh parsley, finely chopped

Quinoa patty:

1 cup cooked quinoa, both white and black

1 cup cooked brown rice

½ cup basil leaves, shredded

½ cup fresh parsley, finely chopped

¼ cup chives, finely chopped

salt and ground black pepper

¼ cup sunflower seeds

¼ cup pumpkin seeds

¼ cup sesame seeds, preferably white

1 tablespoon black cumin seeds

Serves 2-4 | 50 minutes

Method

Roasted vegetables:

1. Preheat the oven to 180°C.
2. In a large bowl, toss the vegetables with the herbs and olive oil until they are well coated. Season with salt and pepper.
3. Arrange the vegetables in a single layer on a baking sheet or large roasting dish and bake until they are caramelised and tender, about 25 minutes.

Quinoa Patty:

1. Combine the cooked quinoa and brown rice in a large bowl. Add the fresh basil, parsley and chives.
2. Add the roasted vegetables to the quinoa mixture and blend the ingredients with your hands, slightly mashing them to make the binding for the grains. Season with salt and pepper.
3. Form the mixture into patties of a size you prefer. Generally, a patty of 180g is sufficient for a meal.
4. Combine the sunflower, pumpkin, sesame and cumin seeds in a small plate. Gently but firmly coat each side of each patty in the seed mixture.
5. Serve the patties cold or at room temperature. You can also heat them in a 150°C oven for 20 minutes.

Tip

For a light lunch, serve a vegetable patty with beetroot salad and macadamia pesto, or with steamed vegetables. You can also break the patties up and serve them in a wrap or as an accompaniment to a meal with steamed fish or grilled chicken.

Nutritional Information:

The combination of quinoa, brown rice and the seeds is so packed with nutrients it's hard to name one that isn't in this recipe. Because this patty is rich in protein, it is quite filling just as it is, but it can always be combined with animal protein to go from a nutritious lunch to satisfying and filling dinner with the addition of simple greens.

Extra Green Frittata

Extra Green Frittata

Ingredients

1 small stalk broccoli, stems trimmed, finely chopped

1 large spring onion, finely sliced

½ head silver beet, stems trimmed, finely sliced

1 bunch parsley, finely chopped

½ cup fresh basil, julienned

8 large eggs

1 cup almond milk

3 small zucchini, thinly sliced

olive oil to drizzle

salt and ground black pepper

Serves 6-8 | 40 minutes

Tip

Serve with macadamia pesto and a drizzle of maple-balsamic dressing.

Method

1. Preheat the oven to 160°C.
2. Toss all the greens, herbs and vegetables — except for the zucchini — in a large bowl then transfer them to a deep baking dish.
3. Beat the eggs with the almond milk and pour over the ingredients in the baking dish. You may need to press the vegetables down with your hands so that they are evenly soaked with the egg.
4. Arrange the zucchini slices over the top of the frittata and drizzle with olive oil. Season with salt and pepper. Bake in the hot oven until firm, about 20 to 25 minutes.

Nutritional Information:

This frittata is good at any time of the day... as a breakfast, lunch or after-school snack, served hot or cold. It will increase your vegetable consumption and provide protein from the eggs, as well as numerous vitamins and minerals from all the vegetables. Great to keep in the fridge ready to go!

Quinoa Fried Rice

Quinoa Fried Rice

Ingredients

Quinoa:

1 teaspoon fresh ginger, peeled and grated

1 large clove garlic, minced

1 teaspoon coconut oil

2 small carrots, peeled and thinly sliced

½ medium red capsicum, seeded and thinly sliced

1 large head broccoli, roughly chopped

1 cup red cabbage, shredded

2–4 tablespoons filtered water

1 cup sprouted mung beans

1 cup cooked quinoa

extra mung beans and wedges of lime, optional

Dressing:

2 tablespoons tamari

1 teaspoon maple syrup

½ teaspoon fresh red chili, seeded and finely chopped

½ cup assorted fresh herbs, chopped — try Thai basil, coriander and mint

Serves 3-4 | 30 minutes

Method

Quinoa:

1. Heat a large skillet or wok over medium heat and sauté the ginger and garlic in coconut oil until they are fragrant but not brown.
2. Add the carrots, capsicum, broccoli and red cabbage. Stir-fry until the vegetables soften. Add the water to prevent them from sticking.
3. Stir in the mung beans and cooked quinoa. When they are heated through, stir in the dressing and fresh herbs. Serve with the extra mung beans and lime wedges if desired.

Dressing:

1. Whisk together the tamari and maple syrup. Add the red chili and stir to combine. Keep covered and chilled until ready to use.

Nutritional Information:

Quinoa is a nutrient-dense seed that is usually used as a grain would be used in recipes. It is high in protein and minerals and combines well with the highly alkalising vegetables and warming spices. You can always add more vegetables for an even greater nutrient content.

Green Lentil Tabouli with White Fish

Green Lentil Tabouli with White Fish

Ingredients

Lentils:

1 cup French (Puy) green lentils

1 bay leaf

3 cups filtered water

Salad:

1 cup cherry tomatoes

1 ¼ cup fresh mint leaves

2 ¼ cups fresh parsley, finely chopped

1 small cucumber, finely chopped

Dressing:

juice of 2 lemons

½ teaspoon maple syrup

3 tablespoons of olive oil

salt and ground black pepper

Fish:

1–2 fillets of white fish, such as snapper, blue cod or gurnard

salt and ground black pepper

2 tablespoons coconut oil

Method

Lentils:

1. Rinse the lentils in a sieve. Put them in a medium saucepan with the bay leaf and the water. Bring the water to a boil, remove any impurities that come to the surface, then lower the heat and simmer until they are cooked.

Salad:

1. Halve the cherry tomatoes, or quarter them if they are large.
2. Tear the mint leaves
3. Combine the salad ingredients with the cooked lentils.

Dressing:

1. Whisk together the lemon juice, maple syrup, and the olive oil. Season with salt and pepper.
2. Toss the dressing with the lentils and salad ingredients. Set the tabouli aside in the refrigerator until ready to use.

Fish:

1. Season the fish with the salt and pepper. Heat the coconut oil in a small skillet over medium heat.
2. Sauté the fish for about 2 ½ minutes on each side. It should be just cooked through and flake easily when pressed with a fork.
3. Place the sautéed fish on top of the tabouli and serve with additional steamed greens if desired.

Serves 2-3 | 25 minutes

Nutritional Information:

The combination of the lentil tabouli and lightly sautéed fish is not only refreshing and delicious, it's especially easy on the digestive system. The fish and lentils provide protein, while the parsley is a major contributor of chlorophyll to make your blood happy, and also includes iron and other minerals.

Quinoa Sushi

Quinoa Sushi

Ingredients

Sushi:

1 cup of mixed-colour quinoa, cooked

3 sheets of nori

1 carrot, julienned

1 spring onion, green part only, thinly sliced

½ medium red capsicum, seeded and thinly sliced

1 small beetroot, peeled and julienned

¼ cup of sesame seeds

Sushi Dressing:

1 tablespoon rice vinegar or apple cider vinegar

1 ½ teaspoons maple syrup

1 tablespoon tahini (unhulled if possible)

juice of ½ lemon

1 tablespoon fresh ginger, peeled and grated

Method

1. Whisk together all the ingredients for the sushi dressing until well combined.
2. Mix the warm cooked quinoa and the dressing in a large bowl, blending until the quinoa becomes sticky. Cover the bowl and let the quinoa sit to absorb the flavours.

To assemble:

1. Wet your hands and lay the 3 nori sheets on a work surface.
2. Spread the seasoned quinoa evenly over ¾ of each sheet.
3. Arrange the carrot, spring onion, capsicum and beetroot segments in the middle. Sprinkle with sesame seeds then roll each sheet, starting from an end that has been spread with quinoa and finishing with the end of the nori that was left unfilled. Use a little water if necessary to seal the seam.
4. Place the rolls, seam-side down, on a clean work surface and cut each roll into 6–8 pieces.

Serves 3-4 | 30 minutes

Nutritional Information:

Nori is a beneficial addition to the diet due to its high fibre and mineral content. Nori is a good source of iodine, which is essential for thyroid, breast, ovary and vascular health. Quinoa is a good source of protein, fibre and minerals and is a nourishing alternative to white rice.

Brown Rice Sushi

Brown Rice Sushi

Ingredients

Sushi:

5 to 10 pieces of pumpkin, cut into 2cm x 10cm strips and baked.

1 teaspoon coconut oil

salt and ground black pepper

1 cup brown rice, cooked

3 sheets nori

1 red capsicum, seeded and thinly sliced

1 medium cucumber, peeled and sliced into lengths

3 garlic sprouts or chives, cut lengthwise into segments

1 large carrot, peeled and finely julienned

¼ cup white sesame seeds or other seed mixture

Sushi Dressing:

1 tablespoon rice wine vinegar or apple cider vinegar

1 ½ teaspoon maple syrup

1 tablespoon tahini (unhulled if possible)

juice of ½ lemon

1 tablespoon fresh ginger, peeled and grated

Method

1. Preheat the oven to 180°C.
2. Coat pumpkin in coconut oil, season and bake in a hot oven until tender.
3. Whisk together all the ingredients for the sushi dressing until well combined.
4. Mix the warm cooked rice and the dressing in a large bowl, blending until the rice becomes sticky. Cover the bowl and let the rice sit to absorb the flavours.

To assemble:

1. Wet your hands and lay the 3 nori sheets on a work surface.
2. Spread the seasoned rice evenly over ¾ of each sheet.
3. Arrange the pumpkin, capsicum, cucumber, garlic sprouts and carrot in the middle. Sprinkle with sesame seeds then roll each sheet, starting from an end that has been spread with rice and finishing with the end of the nori that was left unfilled. Use a little water if necessary to seal the seam.
4. Place the rolls, seam-side down, on a clean work surface and cut each roll into 12 pieces.

Serves 3-4 | 30 minutes

Nutritional Information:

Nori is made from kelp, a seaweed naturally high in iodine. This trace mineral is essential for the conversion of thyroid hormones into their active form. Iodine is not only crucial for healthy thyroid function but also for breast, ovary and vascular health.

Green Open Sandwich

Green Open Sandwich

Ingredients

Sandwich:

1 tablespoon coconut oil

1 bunch baby spinach or silver beet, roughly chopped

½ cup button mushrooms or field mushrooms, roughly chopped

½ cup fresh broccoli, sliced

1 red capsicum, seeded and finely sliced

1 leek, sliced and washed

salt and ground black pepper

1 bunch kale, finely chopped

1 large egg, hard boiled and sliced

1 slice Essene bread

live sprouts and chopped flat-leaf parsley for garnish, optional

Dressing:

1 tablespoon tahini (unhulled if possible)

juice of 1 lemon

1 teaspoon maple syrup

Serves 1 | 15 minutes

Method

1. Heat the coconut oil in a large skillet and sauté the spinach, mushrooms, broccoli, capsicum and leek. Cook until the vegetables are just wilted, then season with the salt and pepper.
2. Whisk together the tahini, lemon juice and maple syrup in a medium bowl. Add the chopped kale and stir the kale around until it is slightly softened. Set aside.

To assemble:

1. Arrange the slices of cooked egg on the piece of bread. Spoon the sautéed vegetables over the egg.
2. Top the vegetables with the dressed kale.
   Serve with the sprouts and parsley if desired.

Note

The Essene bread is quite crumbly and can be difficult to cut. It may be best to serve this open sandwich on a large plate. Toasting the bread will lower its nutrient content. If Essene bread is not available, look for a bread or rolls made of live sprouts, sometime referred to as raw bread.

Nutritional Information:

Serving kale raw optimises its dense nutritional value. It is a powerhouse of dietary fibre, vitamins and minerals. Highly alkaline, this nourishing sandwich is perfect for a lunch that will sustain you for hours.

Ginger Cashew Vegetable Fried Rice

Ginger Cashew Vegetable Fried Rice

Ingredients

macadamia oil for stir-frying

2 tablespoons of fresh ginger, peeled and grated

1 clove garlic, minced

¾ cup broccoli florets

1 stalk celery, peeled and chopped

1 cup green cabbage, shredded

5 mushrooms, chopped

salt and ground black pepper

⅓ cup filtered water

2 tablespoons tamari

¼ cup raw cashews

1 ½ cups brown rice, cooked

¼ cup fresh coriander, chopped

1 teaspoon pumpkin seeds

1 teaspoon sunflower seeds

1 teaspoon white sesame seeds

1 teaspoon black sesame seeds

Serves 2-3 | 25 minutes

Method

1. Heat a little macadamia oil in a large skillet over medium heat. Sauté the ginger and garlic until fragrant, not brown.
2. Add the broccoli, celery, cabbage, mushrooms and season with salt and pepper. Stir-fry a few minutes until the vegetables soften, then add the water to the skillet and let the vegetables steam until the water is evaporated.
3. Add the tamari and cashews, then stir in the cooked brown rice. Mix well and serve with the fresh coriander sprinkled on top with the seeds.

Tip

To make a complete meal, serve this dish with grilled fish, chicken or beef added. A sprinkling of hot chili adds a spicy kick.

Nutritional Information:

This recipe is a much healthier alternative to typical Asian-style takeaway, often higher in white rice than vegetable content. The vegetables in this dish are packed with minerals and other nutrients. The seeds not only add crunch but they also contain magnesium and zinc, while ginger is great for digestion. Brown rice provides a good source of dietary fibre and additional minerals.

Roast Vegetable Crumble

Ingredients

Vegetable Filling:
1 cup quinoa

2 cups filtered water

2 cups pumpkin, peeled and cubed

1 small red capsicum, seeded and cubed

1 small yellow capsicum, seeded and cubed

1 large carrot, finely diced

½ sweet potato, peeled and cubed

salt and ground black pepper

pinch of cinnamon

2 tablespoons coconut oil

Cashew Cheese Sauce:
2 cups raw cashew nuts

1 ½ cups filtered water

pinch turmeric

2 teaspoons Dijon mustard

2 tablespoons savoury yeast

salt and ground black pepper

Parsley Crust:
1 ¼ cups gluten-free bread crumbs

half a bunch parsley, finely chopped

1 garlic clove, minced

pinch of cinnamon

salt and ground black pepper

2 tablespoons olive oil

Method

Cashew Cheese Sauce:
1. Blend all ingredients in a blender until smooth and resembling a thick sauce.

Parsley crust:
1. Combine all parsley crust ingredients together in a bowl.
2. Mix well to combine oil evenly.
3. Set aside until just before baking.

Vegetable Filling:
1. Cook quinoa in water via the absorption method.
2. Season vegetables with salt and pepper and a pinch of cinnamon.
3. Toss with coconut oil and roast in the oven at 170°C until vegetables are cooked.

Assembly:
1. Mix cooked quinoa and vegetables together and add to a 25cm baking tin.
2. Spoon cashew cheese sauce over quinoa and vegetable mixture.
3. Sprinkle parsley crust over vegetable mixture.
4. Bake in the oven at 170°C until warm right through and the crust is slightly crunchy.

Serves 4-5 | 55 minutes

Nutritional Information:

This delicious and warming dish can be served with a pile of greens and/or a fist size of additional protein. The gooey texture from the cashew cheese and the crunch of the parsley crust make this vegetable bake like no other. Dairy-free and gluten-free, this bake is packed full of goodness, including monounsaturated fat, beneficial to heart health.

Green Split Pea and Potato Cakes

Green Split Pea and Potato Cakes

Ingredients

1 cup green split peas

3 ¼ cups filtered water

2 cups Agria potato, peeled and cubed

½ tablespoon curry powder

½ teaspoon cumin

1 teaspoon green chili, seeded and finely chopped (optional)

½ cup fresh coriander, chopped

¼ cup spring onions, finely sliced

¼ cup currants

salt and ground black pepper

½–1 cup of gluten-free breadcrumbs

2 tablespoons coconut oil for frying

Method

1. In a saucepan, heat water and split peas; boil until soft. Drain water and mash lightly.
2. In a separate pot, cover potato cubes with water and bring to the boil. Cook until soft, but not falling apart.
3. In a large mixing bowl combine drained cooked potato and split peas with spices, herbs, spring onions and currants. Add salt and pepper to taste. Mash mixture with hands until ingredients are evenly distributed. Mixture is quite wet, but don't panic. Gently form into balls and flatten to 1 ¼ centimetres thick.
4. Place your breadcrumbs on a plate. Place patties on crumbs and gently cover tops of patties with more crumbs. In a fry pan, heat coconut oil for frying. Cook patties until golden, approximately 5 minutes each side.

Serves 3-4 | 45 minutes | Freezer-friendly

Tip

Mixture can also be used as a mash or a topping for a pie. Mixture is freezable.

Nutritional Information:

These Indian-inspired potato cakes have the benefits of warming spices, known in traditional medicines to assist digestive function. Green split peas are a good source of protein, fibre and minerals adding to the nutritional value of these very yummy potato cakes.

Brown Rice Salad

Ingredients

1 tablespoon coconut oil

1 small carrot, peeled and finely diced

1 spring onion, finely sliced

½ cup red cabbage, shredded

⅓ cup peas (fresh or frozen)

1 cup long-grain brown rice, cooked and sprinkled with turmeric

¼ cup buckwheat groats

¼ cup currants

¼ cup fresh coriander, chopped

1 cup cucumber, peeled and diced

1 tablespoon red chili, seeded and finely chopped

salt and ground black pepper

Serves 3-4 | 25 minutes

Method

1. Heat the coconut oil in a medium saucepan and stir-fry the carrot, spring onion, cabbage, and peas until the cabbage wilts.
2. Take the pan off the heat and add the cooked rice, buckwheat, currants and fresh coriander.
3. Stir in the cucumber and chili, then season with salt and pepper.

Tip

This dish can be served warm or chilled.
Try it with braised lamb, grilled fish, or a large field mushroom, such as a Portobello, and simply steamed greens.

Nutritional Information:

Since the process of producing brown rice removes only the hull of the kernel, it is an excellent source of minerals and dietary fibre. This Moroccan-style rice is delicious on its own or with a small portion of additional protein, if that appeals. I love mine with a sprinkling of mixed seeds for extra minerals and crunch.

Rice Paper Rolls with Quinoa

RICE PAPER ROLLS WITH QUINOA

INGREDIENTS

2 cups quinoa
4 cups filtered water
salt and ground black pepper
1 bunch fresh mint
½ bunch Thai basil
1 carrot, shredded
1 cucumber, thinly sliced
1 red capsicum, seeded and finely sliced
1 spring onion, finely sliced
¼ cup raw macadamia nuts, chopped
1 tablespoon sesame seeds
1 packet rice paper rolls
½ avocado, sliced

METHOD

1. Cook quinoa in water via the absorption method.
2. While quinoa is still warm, season with salt and pepper and allow to cool.
3. Remove leaves from mint and basil.
4. Mix herbs and all remaining ingredients, except rice paper rolls and avocado, with cooked quinoa until combined.

ASSEMBLY:

1. Fill a large bowl with warm water.
2. Dip one sheet of rice paper into the water until it softens, and then lay it flat on a plate.
3. Place approximately ⅓ cup of quinoa mix into the centre of the rice paper.
4. Place 2 slices of avocado on top of quinoa mixture.
5. Fold the sides into the centre over the filling, then the bottom of the paper up and over (tucking the bottom of the roll in). Roll from bottom to top to form a tight roll.
6. Set aside and continue until all ingredients are finished.

Serves 8-10 | 45 minutes

NUTRITIONAL INFORMATION:

Quinoa was once called the gold of the Incas and it's easy to see why. It contains all of the essential amino acids, making it a complete protein and a good choice for vegans. It has a significant amount of the amino acid lysine, which is used for tissue growth and repair. The addition of the raw macadamia nuts provides a delightful crunch and mineral boost. This is a delicious way to eat your vegetables!

Pumpkin and Sweet potato Fritters

Pumpkin and Sweet potato Fritters

Ingredients

1 ½ cups sweet potato, grated

½ cup pumpkin, grated

2 spring onions or ½ large brown onion, finely chopped

1 cup flat-leaf parsley, finely chopped

1 cup spelt flour

salt and ground black pepper

olive oil or coconut oil for frying

Serves 3-4 | 35 minutes

Method

1. Combine sweet potato, pumpkin, spring onion and parsley.
2. Add flour, salt and pepper and massage into the sweet potato and pumpkin mix. Squeeze the mixture in your hands to allow a bind to form naturally.
3. Form small patties between hands. Mixture is quite wet.
4. Heat enough oil to coat a pan.
5. Gently fry fritters on medium heat until golden, turning once. Cook for approximately 6 minutes each side.

Tip

Rice flour can be substituted for spelt flour to make these fritters gluten-free.

Nutritional Information:

These fritters could be called "vision fritters" as they contain two good sources of beta-carotene, which the body converts into Vitamin A, vital for eye health. Try these fritters with a side of Beetroot and Almond Salad (p.143) for a satisfying lunch.

LET FOOD BE THY MEDICINE
AND MEDICINE BE THY FOOD.
— HIPPOCRATES

Why Eat The RFC Way?

- To increase the nutrient content of the diet through a high-plant diet.
- To support optimal blood pH by providing practical ways to include more green vegetables in meals.
- To decrease the synthetic chemical load being consumed by encouraging the use of organic food.
- To enhance and support detoxification processes through omitting "liver loaders" and supplying the nutrients necessary to optimise these functions.
- To support the energy systems of the body through optimal nutrient intake while lowering the intake of substances that can interfere with the creation of energy.

The most powerful force on Earth
is the human soul on fire.

Get fired up about amping up your nutrition!

— Dr Libby

Beetroot and Almond Salad (p.141)

Snacks

Nut Butter Muffins (p.143)

Apple Salad with Sweet and Sour Dressing (p.147)

Cashew Nut Hot Chocolate (p.153)

Simple Chocolate Truffles (p.151)

Snacks

Exploring the history of food helps guide us with what to eat, especially when it comes to managing insulin levels. The only carbohydrates human once ate were legumes, pulses, and berries. These days, there are over 3000 snack-food items alone on the average supermarket's shelves, and this number is growing constantly. These packaged foods are what I call "high human intervention" (high HI) foods, highly modified from their original food source and a far cry from the way nature guides us to eat.

Real food decomposes so it is only with the addition of additives, preservatives, refined sugar or salt that these "foods" can last on the shelf for any length of time. Our bodies thrive on being supplied with living foods, so the more we can incorporate plants into our diet the better we feel!

This Snacks section can literally help you transform your day. I so often find it is snack foods where people get stuck. They can start with a nourishing breakfast, grab whatever they can for lunch, and then all of a sudden the 3pm sugar cravings kick in and any bar of chocolate, packet of lollies, cookie, muffin or coffee stall better be ready!

Being organised and having home-made snacks ready and available can truly change your health. Taking your own snacks with you might become a new non-negotiable for you most or every day of the week.

We've designed these snacks to be easily prepared and accessed. Sunday can be a great day to sit down and plan out lunches and snacks if you feel that will help you. Most of these options can be frozen and taken out for individual use (with the exception of the salads.) So you may want to consider making a few batches and then freezing them to have on hand so you rely less on their pre-packaged counterparts that contain far fewer nutrients and usually other added non-food ingredients.

Carrot Cake with Coconut and Cashew Icing

Carrot Cake with Coconut and Cashew Icing

Ingredients

Cake:

2 cups raw walnuts, halves and pieces

2 cups desiccated coconut

½ teaspoon ground cinnamon

pinch ground nutmeg

¼ teaspoon ground ginger

2 tablespoons psyllium powder

3 large carrots, peeled and grated

4 Medjool dates, pitted and coarsely chopped

¼ cup maple syrup

½ cup currants

zest of 1 lemon

zest of 1 orange

Icing:

1 ½ cups fresh coconut flesh

½ cup raw cashews

¼ cup coconut water

1 tablespoon maple syrup

1 large lemon, juiced and zest grated

Method

Cake:

1. Combine the walnuts, coconut, cinnamon, nutmeg, ginger and psyllium powder in the bowl of a food processor. Pulse until the mixture resembles a fine crumb. Set this mixture aside.
2. Combine the grated carrots, dates and maple syrup in the bowl of the food processor. Pulse until the mixture is well blended, scraping down the sides of the bowl if necessary.
3. Stir the carrot mixture with the spice mixture until well blended.
4. Fold in the currants and zest of the lemon and orange. Stir to blend well.
5. Line a 30cm loaf pan with baking paper. Transfer the cake mixture into the pan, pressing it firmly into all corners. Smooth the top with a spatula and refrigerate it for about 30 minutes.

Icing:

1. Combine the coconut flesh and cashew nuts in a blender. Blend until the coconut is well chopped and the nuts are well ground.
2. Add the coconut water, maple syrup, lemon juice and zest to the mixture and blend until smooth and creamy.

To Assemble:

1. Invert the chilled cake onto a large platter and remove the baking paper from the bottom of the cake.
2. Generously spread the top and sides of the cake with the coconut icing. Chill the frosted cake until the icing hardens. Please keep the cake refrigerated.

Serves 10 | 35 minutes | Freezer-friendly

Nutritional Information:

An unbaked cake is nutritionally superior to the traditional baked version as all vitamins are retained. Carrots supply essential beta-carotene, required for healthy vision. The cake is also a source of anti-inflammatory omega-3 fatty acids, thanks to the walnuts. The coconut and cashew icing is so creamy and nutrient-dense. Eat it slowly and savour every bite!

Beetroot and Almond Salad

Beetroot and Almond Salad

Ingredients

Salad:

1 bunch baby spinach leaves, about 1 cup

1 cup fresh mint

1 cup fresh parsley, leaves only

¼ cup raw almonds, soaked in water overnight, then rinsed well

1 cup baby beetroots, peeled and julienned

Dressing:

2 tablespoons flaxseed oil

1 tablespoon apple cider vinegar

1 tablespoon maple syrup

juice of 1 large orange

salt and ground black pepper

Serves 1-2 | 10 minutes

Method

1. Combine the spinach, mint and parsley in a large bowl. Drain the almonds and add to the bowl.
2. Add the beetroot to the salad and set-aside until ready to serve.

Sauce:

1. Whisk together the flaxseed oil and vinegar. Stir in the maple syrup and the orange juice. Season with salt and black pepper.
2. Toss the salad with the dressing and serve on chilled plates.

Nutritional Information:

Enhance detoxification and digestion simultaneously with this sparkling salad packed with nutrient-dense ingredients. Beetroots benefit the liver, aiding in detoxification. The herbs and greens do their part as well and the splash of apple cider vinegar also aids the digestion-support properties of this super-healthy combination. This dish is an ideal addition to any meal or perfect as a pick-me-up snack.

Nut Butter Muffins

NUT BUTTER MUFFINS

INGREDIENTS

1 cup organic nut butter — peanut, almond or cashew

2 small bananas, peeled and smashed

2 large eggs, well beaten

½ teaspoon baking powder

1 teaspoon apple cider vinegar

1 cup blueberries (fresh or frozen)

METHOD

1. Preheat the oven to 180°C.
2. Grind the nut butter in a blender until it is smooth.
3. Add the bananas and beaten eggs to the smooth nut mixture and combine until they are well incorporated.
4. Add the baking powder and apple cider vinegar to the dough and blend until well mixed.
5. Remove the dough from the blender and gently fold in the blueberries.
6. Spoon the batter into 12 individual muffin cups and bake in the preheated oven for 10 minutes.

Makes 12 | 20 minutes | Freezer-friendly

NUTRITIONAL INFORMATION:

Gluten- and dairy-free muffins are yummo! These luscious muffins not only burst with a nutty flavor, the blueberries and bananas add antioxidants, vitamin E and potassium. Try these when you feel like the texture of baked goods, while knowing you are investing in your health.

Brain Balls

Brain Balls

Ingredients

2 cups raw walnuts, halves and pieces

1 cup sunflower seeds

8 Medjool dates, pitted
and coarsely chopped

1 cup desiccated coconut

⅔ cup cocoa powder

pinch of salt

¼ cup filtered water

Method

1. Combine all ingredients in a food processor and process until the mixture forms a dough. Add a little extra water if needed to ensure it is well combined.
2. Form the dough into medium-sized balls by rolling a portion between your palms. Place the finished balls on a tray lined with waxed paper or in a container and chill for at least 30 minutes before serving.

Makes 14-16 | 15 minutes | Freezer-friendly

Nutritional Information:

This chewy, nutty snack is an excellent source of the monounsaturated fats and omega-3 fatty acids that have the anti-inflammatory properties so necessary for a healthy heart and optimal brain function. Keep these easy-to-make snacks on hand for the perfect after-school snack for a burst of energy or as a source of vitamin E and zinc, beneficial for skin and the immune system.

Apple Salad with Sweet and Sour Dressing

Apple Salad with Sweet and Sour Dressing

Ingredients

Salad:

1 large apple, such as Fuji, Gala, Granny Smith or Braeburn

juice of 1 lemon

1 cup fresh mung beans

½ cup raw walnuts, chopped

Dressing:

2 Medjool dates, pitted and coarsely chopped

2 teaspoons mustard seeds, finely ground

2 teaspoons fresh ginger, peeled and grated

1 teaspoon apple cider vinegar

juice of 1 lemon

juice of 1 orange

2 tablespoons olive oil

salt and ground black pepper

Serves 2-3 | 15 minutes

Method

Salad:

1. Core and thinly slice the apple — you can leave the skin on or peel it if you prefer. Sprinkle the apple slices with the fresh lemon juice.
2. Toss the apple with the mung beans and walnuts. Serve with the sweet and sour dressing.

Dressing:

1. Combine all ingredients except the olive oil in a blender and blend to form a thick sauce.
2. With the motor running, pour in the olive oil. Season to taste with the salt and pepper and serve with the apple salad.

Nutritional Information:

Apples are a great source of dietary fibre and this salad is a fresh way to try something new. The apple cider vinegar aids with digestion and the walnuts are an excellent source of anti-inflammatory omega-3 fatty acids. You can also serve this salad as a light lunch with plenty of dark leafy greens and/or additional protein for a highly nutritious meal.

Chocolate Seed Balls

Chocolate Seed Balls

Ingredients

1 ½ cups raw walnuts, halves and pieces

½ cup raw cacao powder

¼ cup whole linseeds

¼ cup sesame seeds

8 Medjool dates, pitted and coarsely chopped

¼ teaspoon vanilla

2 tablespoons filtered water

pinch of salt

desiccated coconut for rolling

Method

1. Combine all ingredients except coconut in a food processor and process until it resembles a dough-like consistancy.
2. Roll into medium-sized balls between your palms and coat with coconut.

Makes 10-12 | 15 minutes | Freezer-friendly

Nutritional Information:

This is the perfect afternoon snack or after-dinner dessert. The healthy fats and protein content mean these truffles are very satiating. Flaxseeds are a good source of omega-3 fatty acids, beneficial for a healthy heart and skin. Just be aware that cacao contains caffeine so if sleep is a challenge, enjoy them earlier in the day.

Simple Chocolate Truffles

Ingredients

⅓ cup cacao powder

¼ cup pumpkin seeds

¼ cup sunflower seeds

½ cup desiccated coconut

pinch salt

8 Medjool dates, pitted and coarsely chopped

¼ cup filtered water

Method

1. Combine the cacoa powder with the seeds in the bowl of a food processor and pulse until combined. Add the coconut and salt and pulse again.
2. Add the chopped dates to the mixture in the processor and pulse until the ingredients begin to form a dough. Add the water to smooth the mixture and pulse for a few more seconds.
3. Roll a portion of the mixture between your palms to form medium-sized balls. If the mixture is crumbling add more water. Lay them on a sheet pan lined with waxed paper. Chill the truffles until ready to use.

Makes 10-12 | 15 minutes | Freezer-friendly

Tip

The truffles can be rolled in cacao nibs, finely chopped pistachio nuts or crushed buckwheat groats for a finishing touch. Be sure to store them carefully so the coatings don't rub off.

Nutritional Information:

A must for a perfect complexion, magnesium and zinc are found in high proportions in pumpkin seeds. These truffles, rich in both of these minerals as well as antioxidants and fibre, make a wonderful and satisfying snack.

Cashew Nut Hot Chocolate

CASHEW NUT HOT CHOCOLATE

INGREDIENTS

1 cup raw cashew nuts

2 cups filtered water

pinch of salt

3 tablespoons maple syrup

¼ cup cacao powder

METHOD

1. Blend ingredients in a high speed blender.
2. Heat over the lowest possible heat on stove until warm. Do not boil.
3. Serve in small espresso glasses as a dessert or as a hot chocolate alternative.

Serves 2-3 | 15 minutes

NUTRITIONAL INFORMATION:

It's hard to believe there is no cream in this silky smooth hot chocolate alternative. Packed with antioxidants and minerals such as calcium and magnesium, a small serve of this liquid delight is perfect for afternoon tea on a cold winter's day... actually all year round!

Eating organic food is not just about what you get — more antioxidants, for example. It's also about the pesticides you omit with that selection.

— Dr Libby

Satay Chicken Salad (p.181)

Dinner

Moussaka (p.173)

Spelt pizza with Macadamia Pesto (p.187)

African Black-eyed Beans (p.207)

Spiced Greens and Lamb Backstrap (p.177)

Dinner

As the final meal of the day, dinner is the ideal opportunity to amp up your greens. Cooking can be quite medicinal if you allow it to be. Instead of focusing on how many people you have to feed, how late it is or what little time you have to prepare the food, stop and think about it. Be grateful for all that you are and all that you have. Consider your dinner meal an opportunity to nourish yourself and those you love and with that in mind, the way you approach food preparation changes.

The human body has around 50 trillion cells that interact with all the organs of the body every minute of every day. If you stop and consider that the meals you make will become part of you, cooking nourishing food becomes even more important. As a gentle reminder, portion size needs to be considered and dinner doesn't need to be the enormous meal it is for many people in the Western world. Around two fist sizes is appropriate for concentrated foods (low-water foods such as proteins and/or carbohydrates) plus plenty of high-water vegetables.

The dinner meal became a ritual around 6pm due to the emergence of the working class who wanted to have something substantial to eat upon returning from work. From a nutritional perspective this is actually a really great time to eat dinner. You are often truly hungry around this time and you will digest your food more effectively eating earlier in the night. I once attended a seminar where the speaker asked, "What time do children and the elderly eat dinner?" The whole room, unprompted, answered, "5 o'clock." One reason for this is that they aren't influenced by work hours. Do what is practical for you. I am simply saying that if you can, eat earlier rather than later.

If you keep your pantry and fridge stocked with the *Real Food Chef* lists, there will always be a meal in the house. For those who go to work, dinner can feel like a stress and just another thing to consider in what seems to be a never-ending day. Have fun with food. Remember why you are choosing to eat this way. These recipes have been created to be adapted, if you want to. Add in your favorite vegetables, spices or nuts and seeds if that appeals.

Never be afraid to add more vegetables, particularly green ones. The focus of the dinner recipes is to provide more inspiration and many different ways of preparing vegetables. Every cell of your body will love you for it.

Green Leaf Burritos with Mexican Kidney Beans

Green Leaf Burritos with Mexican Kidney Beans

Ingredients

Bean Mixture:

2 cups dried kidney beans, soaked in water

2L filtered water

2 tablespoons macadamia nut oil

1 large onion, diced

2 cloves garlic, minced

1 each red, yellow and green capsicum, seeded and diced

1 small red or green chili, seeded and finely chopped

2 400g cans of whole tomatoes

½ cup tomato paste

1 teaspoon salt

3 tablespoons maple syrup

1 tablespoon cacao powder

Burritos:

6 leaves silver beet, tough stems removed

1 cup lettuce, shredded

2 cups fresh tomatoes, chopped

1 cup cooked brown rice, optional

Guacamole:

2 avocados

¼ teaspoon cumin

juice of 1 lime

Salt and ground black pepper

Salsa:

2 fresh tomatoes, chopped

1 each yellow, green and red capsicum, seeded and diced

½ cup fresh coriander, chopped

1 teaspoon ground cumin

juice of 1 lime

Salt and ground black pepper

Cashew Sour Cream:

1 ½ cups raw cashew nuts

juice of 1 lemon

juice of 1 lime

salt to taste

¾ cup filtered water

Serves 3 | 75 minutes

Nutritional Information:

This recipe is packed with vitamins, minerals and phytochemicals... all wrapped up in a bundle! The vegetables are rich in beneficial amounts of folate, lycopene and vitamin C. The kidney beans are an excellent source of dietary fibre to assist with outstanding elimination. The silver beet wraps are significantly higher in nutrients than white flour-based tortillas and contribute to the alkaline power of your daily diet.

Green Leaf Burritos with Mexican Kidney Beans

Method

Bean Mixture:

1. Drain the soaked beans and put them in a large pot with enough water to cover by 4 to 5 centimetres. Bring the pot to a boil, then lower the heat and simmer for 40 to 50 minutes or until the beans are tender. Let them rest in the water until they have cooled.
2. Heat the macadamia oil in a saucepan over medium heat. Add the onion, garlic, capsicums, chili. Sauté the vegetables until they are soft.
3. Add the tinned tomatoes, tomato paste and salt to taste.
4. Add the cooked kidney beans, maple syrup and cacao powder to cut the acidity of the tomatoes.
5. Stir the mixture and bring the pot to a boil, then lower the heat and simmer until the mixture has thickened slightly. Add more of the bean cooking water if the mixture dries out.

Guacamole:

1. Mash the avocados with a fork to break up the flesh.
2. Season the avocado with the cumin, salt, pepper and the lime juice. Continue to mash until the mixture is smooth. Keep chilled until ready to use.

Salsa:

1. Combine the tomatoes and diced capsicums, then add the chopped coriander.
2. Season the mixture with the cumin, lime juice and salt and pepper. Keep chilled until ready to use.

Cashew Sour Cream:

1. Grind the nuts in the bowl of a food processor until finely chopped.
2. Add the lemon and lime juices and season with salt.
3. With the motor running, pour in the water and process until the mixture is smooth and creamy.

To Assemble the Burritos:

1. Position 2 silverbeet leaves with their stem ends overlapping.
2. Spoon some of the bean mixture down the centre of the silver beet leaves. Add the shredded lettuce, chopped tomatoes and the optional brown rice.
3. Roll the leaves up over the filling. Spoon some of the salsa over the middle of the burrito. Top the salsa with a dollop of the guacamole, then drizzle the whole assembly with some of the cashew cream.

Cashew, Cauliflower and Quinoa Sprout Soup

Cashew, Cauliflower and Quinoa Sprout Soup

Ingredients

1 tablespoon olive oil
½ onion, chopped
1 clove garlic, minced
½ head cauliflower, roughly chopped
pinch caraway seeds
salt and ground black pepper
3 ¼ cup vegetable broth or filtered water
½ cup raw cashew nuts
½ cup quinoa sprouts, or other live sprout

Method

1. Heat the olive oil in a medium saucepan and sauté the onion and garlic over medium heat until they are soft.
2. Add the cauliflower and caraway seeds to the pot and season with salt and pepper.
3. Pour in the vegetable broth and bring the pot to a boil for 2 to 3 minutes.
4. Lower the heat and add the cashews. Simmer for about 5 minutes.
5. Let the soup cool then ladle it into a blender and blend until it is smooth and creamy. Serve with the quinoa sprouts.

Serves 4-6 | 45 minutes | Freezer-friendly

Nutritional Information:

As part of the Brassica family, cauliflower enhances liver detoxification processes. It also contains a compound called sulforaphane, which may protect against some cancers. The cashews contribute an array of minerals good for the nervous system including calcium and magnesium as well as texture and a distinct flavor.

Carrot, Cashew and Fresh Corn Soup

Carrot, Cashew and Fresh Corn Soup

Ingredients

3 cobs fresh corn

1kg carrots, peeled and roughly chopped

1 medium sweet potato, peeled and chopped

1 tablespoon fresh ginger, peeled and grated

1 tablespoon ground cumin

½ teaspoon turmeric

1.5L filtered water

¾ cup raw cashew nuts

salt and ground black pepper

Method

1. Remove the kernels from the corn cobs. Cut the cobs in half and reserve them.
2. Combine the carrots, sweet potato, corn and the cobs, ginger, cumin and turmeric in a large saucepan or soup pot.
3. Add the filtered water, cover the pan and bring to a boil. When the carrots are soft, remove the cobs and let the soup cool.
4. Ladle the cooled soup into the jar of a blender, adding ¼ of the cashews with each ladle.
5. Blend the soup, in batches if necessary, until smooth. Season with salt and pepper.
6. Serve hot or at room temperature.

Serves 5-6 | 90 minutes | Freezer-friendly

Nutritional Information:

It may be hard to believe there's no dairy in this rich and velvety soup. The vivid orange color indicates its high content of beta-carotene, necessary for maintaining great vision. Using organic ingredients increases the natural sweetness of this soup, and the spices aid in digestion.

Pad Thai Chicken

Pad Thai Chicken

Ingredients

Chicken:

500g boneless skinless chicken breast

salt and ground black pepper

¼ cup fresh coriander, finely chopped

¼ cup fresh parsley, finely chopped

1 medium red chili, seeded and finely chopped

1 tablespoon macadamia oil

Vegetables and Noodles:

1 tablespoon coconut oil

100g snow peas, julienned

⅛ medium head green cabbage, shredded

1 small zucchini, julienned

½ red capsicum, seeded and thinly sliced

1 medium red chili, seeded and finely chopped (optional)

salt and ground black pepper

1 medium bunch fresh coriander, chopped

3 large eggs, beaten

1 packet kelp noodles

1 medium spring onion, thinly sliced

¼ cup raw macadamia nuts, roughly chopped

Pad Thai Sauce:

1 fresh kaffir lime leaf, finely sliced

1 tablespoon fresh ginger, peeled and grated

1 large clove garlic, minced

1 tablespoon sesame oil

1 tablespoon tamarind paste

½ teaspoon tamari

1 tablespoon apple cider vinegar

1 tablespoon maple syrup

2 teaspoons fresh lemon juice

2 teaspoons fresh lime juice

Serves 4-5 | 35 minutes

Nutritional Information:

This is a delicious and fresh alternative to standard takeaway Pad Thai chicken. Since this version has no added bottled sauces or non-food ingredients, there won't be any "takeaway hangover" to deal with. Kelp noodles are an excellent source of iodine, necessary for healthy thyroid, breast, ovary and vascular function. The green vegetables add an alkalising element helpful for healthy blood. Leave the chicken out and use a nut and seed mix for a vegan version. This could easily become a family favorite!

Pad Thai Chicken

METHOD

1. Preheat the oven to 180°C.
2. Season the chicken breasts with salt and black pepper. Combine the coriander, parsley and red chili. Coat each piece of chicken in the mixture.
3. Heat the macadamia oil in an oven-proof skillet over medium heat. Sauté the breasts for 1 minute per side, then put the pan in the oven. Bake until the chicken is cooked through, about 8 to 9 minutes.
4. Remove the chicken from the pan and let it rest until cool enough to handle, about 5 minutes. Slice the meat against the grain and set aside until ready to use.

WHILE THE CHICKEN IS BAKING, PREPARE THE VEGETABLES AND NOODLES:

1. Heat half the coconut oil in a large skillet or wok over medium heat.
2. Sauté the snow peas, cabbage and zucchini. Add the capsicum and chili, if using. When the vegetables are wilted, season them with salt and ground black pepper. Add the chopped coriander, then set the vegetables aside.
3. Heat the remaining coconut oil in the same skillet and add the eggs. Scramble the eggs until they are just set.
4. Stir in the packet of kelp noodles and let them heat through. Add the cooked vegetables back to the pan with the eggs and noodles. Toss with the spring onion and macadamia nuts.

FOR THE SAUCE:

1. Over a medium to low heat stir-fry the lime leaf, ginger and garlic in sesame oil until fragrant.
2. Whisk together the tamarind, tamari, apple cider vinegar, maple syrup, lemon and lime juice.
3. Stir this mixture into the softened garlic and ginger.
4. Add the Pad Thai sauce to the vegetables and noodles. Serve with the sliced chicken alongside or with the chicken mixed in.

Moussaka

Moussaka

Ingredients

Roasted Vegetables:

5 small zucchini, cut lengthways into several slices

1 large sweet potato, cut lengthways into several slices

¼ pumpkin, cut into long, thin slices

1 tablespoon olive oil

¼ cup fresh parsley, chopped

1 small spring rosemary leaves, chopped

1 sprig thyme, leaves chopped

salt and ground black pepper

200g baby spinach leaves

Tomato sauce:

2 400g cans diced tomatoes

1 cup fresh parsley, chopped

8 tablespoons tomato paste

2 teaspoons maple syrup

salt and ground black pepper

Bolognaise mixture:

1 cup brown lentils, cooked

1 cup quinoa, cooked

1 cup fresh basil leaves, chopped

1 cup fresh parsley, chopped

2 spring onions, finely chopped

1 teaspoon fresh red chili, seeded and finely chopped

Serves 4-6 | 60 minutes

Tip

Serve with a green salad and balsamic-maple syrup dressing and macadamia pesto.

Nutritional Information:

Using thinly sliced vegetables is a great alternative to lasagna in this vegetable-, fibre- and nutrient-dense moussaka. Lentils are low in two essential amino acids, methionine and cysteine, but when combined with quinoa, a seed, the dish presents a complete protein.

Method

Roasted vegetables:

1. Preheat the oven to 170°C.
2. Drizzle the vegetables with olive oil, toss with parsley, rosemary and thyme and season with salt and pepper.
3. Line a baking tray with parchment paper and arrange the vegetables on top. Bake in the hot oven for about 12 minutes, or until tender.

Tomato sauce:

1. Drain the juice from the tomatoes and transfer them to the bowl of a blender.
2. Add the chopped parsley, tomato paste and maple syrup and season with salt and pepper. Pulse until well blended.

For the bolognaise mixture:

1. Combine the cooked lentils and cooked quinoa in a large bowl and toss with the basil, parsley, spring onion and fresh chili.
2. Stir in 2 cups of the tomato sauce and mix until well blended.

To assemble the moussaka:

1. Lightly oil a 24cm x 14cm baking pan.
2. Start with a layer of sweet potato slices then add half of the spinach. Cover them with 2 ½ cups of the quinoa-lentil mixture.
3. Next layer the zucchini and any leftover sweet potato slices and spinach.
4. Spoon a thin layer of the remaining quinoa-lentil mixture over the zucchini. Top with a layer of the pumpkin slices, pressing firmly.
5. Bake the moussaka in the oven for about 35 minutes to heat through. Let it rest for about 10 minutes before serving.

Ginger Sesame Beans with White Fish

Ginger Sesame Beans with White Fish

Ingredients

Green Beans and Fish:

250g fresh green beans

2 teaspoons coconut oil

4 thin slices fresh ginger, peeled, julienned

1 small red chili, seeded and finely chopped, optional

1–2 fillets of white fish, such as cod, sole or snapper

salt and ground black pepper

Dressing:

1 tablespoon tamari

1 teaspoon maple syrup

¼ teaspoon sesame oil

Method

Green Beans and Fish:

1. Bring a small pot of salted water to a boil and blanch the green beans for 4 or 5 minutes. Drain and cool under running water.
2. Heat half the coconut oil in a small skillet and sauté the ginger and red chill until soft and fragrant.
3. Add the green beans to the skillet, toss with the dressing and set aside.
4. Season the fish with the salt and pepper. Heat the remaining coconut oil in a small skillet and sauté the fish about 2 ½ minutes per side. The fish should be opaque in the centre and flake easily when lightly pressed with a fork.
5. Centre the green beans and top with the cooked fish. Serve with additional steamed greens if desired.

Dressing:

1. Whisk together the tamari, maple syrup and sesame oil. Pour over the green beans and toss to mix well.

Serves 1-2 | 15 minutes

Nutritional Information:

Depending on the fat content, fish contains the fat-soluble vitamins A, D and E as well as minerals such as phosphorous and selenium. The green beans are an excellent source of minerals and dietary fibre. This dish is perfect for those who follow food-combining principles.

Spiced Greens and Lamb Backstrap

SPICED GREENS AND LAMB BACKSTRAP

INGREDIENTS

GREENS:

2 tablespoons olive oil

1 clove garlic, minced

1 teaspoon red chili, seeded and finely chopped

1 cup peas (fresh or frozen)

1 large bunch silver beet, tough stems removed

juice of ½ lemon

1 fresh tomato, chopped

salt and ground black pepper

LAMB:

2 tablespoons olive oil

1 tablespoon red chili, seeded and finely chopped

1 clove garlic, minced

¼ cup fresh parsley, finely chopped

1 lamb backstrap

2 tablespoons spelt flour, or other wholegrain flour

Serves 2-3 | 25 minutes

METHOD

GREENS:

1. Gently heat the oil in a small saucepan with the garlic and chili.
2. Add the peas and heat through for about a minute.
3. Chop the silver beet and add it to the peas. Let the leaves wilt, and toss them gently with the mixture.
4. Squeeze lemon over the greens, sprinkle with the chopped tomato and season with salt and pepper.

LAMB:

1. Combine half the oil, chili, garlic and parsley in a zip-lock bag.
2. Toss the lamb in the bag until it's evenly coated. Add the flour to the bag and shake.
3. Heat the remaining oil in a medium skillet over medium to high heat and sear the lamb for 2 to 3 minutes on each side. Remove it to a warm platter and cover with aluminium foil and rest for 5 minutes.
4. Slice the lamb and serve with the greens.

NOTE

These greens can be served with moussaka or as the base of a breakfast with a poached or hard-boiled egg on top. The lamb can also be grilled or finished in a hot oven if you prefer it more well-done.

NUTRITIONAL INFORMATION:

Organic lamb is a rich source of heme iron and zinc. Choose organic, pasture-fed animal protein whenever possible, if you include it in your diet. Served with alkalising greens, this dinner is perfect for those who follow the food-combining concept.

Use-Up-Your-Greens Pasta

Use-Up-Your-Greens Pasta

Ingredients

2 cups organic pasta

3 tablespoons macadamia nut oil

1 head broccoli, stem trimmed, sliced

½ leek, white part only, sliced and rinsed

1 large green capsicum, seeded and finely sliced

1 clove garlic, minced

1 bunch kale, stems removed, chopped

1 large spring onion

1 cup peas (fresh or frozen)

4 tablespoons filtered water

salt and ground black pepper

½ cup fresh basil, shredded

½ cup fresh parsley, chopped

Serves 3-4 | 35 minutes

Method

1. Fill a large pot with salted water. When it comes to a boil, cook the pasta until al dente. Drain it and keep it warm.
2. Heat the macadamia oil in a large skillet over medium heat and sauté the broccoli, leek, capsicum and garlic until they have softened.
3. Add the kale, spring onion and peas. When kale has cooked down, add the water to steam the vegetables and to keep them from sticking. Season the mixture with salt and pepper.
4. Toss the vegetables with the cooked pasta, then add the fresh basil and parsley. Stir all the ingredients to mix them well.

Note

This is not so much a pasta dish as it is a means of increasing your vegetable intake. It can be served cold, room temperature or warm, and a little of the macadamia basil pesto would be an excellent choice to highlight the flavours of this dish.

Nutritional Information:

The vegetables are the stars of this show. This recipe is nutrient-dense and filled with vitamins and minerals. The addition of the pasta makes it ideal for those who follow the concept of food combining. To make it gluten-free, replace the organic pasta with kelp noodles, brown rice or gluten-free pasta.

Satay Chicken Salad

SATAY CHICKEN SALAD

INGREDIENTS

CHICKEN:

500g boneless skinless chicken breast

salt and ground black pepper

¼ cup fresh parsley, finely chopped

¼ cup fresh coriander, finely chopped

1 tablespoon red chili, seeded and finely chopped

1 tablespoon macadamia oil

SALAD:

1 packet kelp noodles

1 bunch fresh kale, stems removed, leaves chopped

1 cup mung bean sprouts

150g snow peas, julienned

1 large carrot, peeled and julienned

½ medium green capsicum, seeded and thinly sliced

1 cup fresh mint

1 cup fresh Thai basil

1 cup fresh coriander

SATAY SAUCE:

1 cup raw cashew nuts

¼ cup organic almond butter

1 tablespoon red chili, seeded and finely chopped

1 tablespoon sesame oil

2 tablespoons fresh ginger, peeled and grated

1 tablespoon maple syrup

2 tablespoons tamari

¼ cup filtered water

Serves 4-5 | 35 minutes

NUTRITIONAL INFORMATION:

Kelp noodles are a mineral-dense alternative to pasta. The variety of different-coloured, plant-based foods in this dish brings a range of antioxidants. Studies show that variety is vital to longevity!

Satay Chicken Salad

METHOD

CHICKEN:

1. Preheat the oven to 180°C.
2. Season the chicken with the salt and pepper. Evenly coat the breast in a mixture of the parsley, coriander, and chili.
3. Heat the macadamia oil in a small oven-proof skillet over medium heat. Sauté the chicken for about 1 minute per side.
4. Put the chicken in the oven, or transfer it to a baking dish, and bake for 8 to 9 minutes, until cooked through. Let it rest for about 5 minutes before slicing it.

SALAD:

1. Combine the kelp noodles with the chopped kale, sprouts, snow peas, carrot and capsicum.
2. Toss the salad with the satay sauce, then add the mint, basil and coriander. Blend all the ingredients until they are well mixed.
3. Serve with the sliced chicken on top or on the side.

SATAY SAUCE:

1. Combine all satay ingredients in a blender except for the water.
2. With the motor running, pour in enough water to make the sauce smooth and creamy. For more texture, don't process the sauce as much. Taste and add more chili if you like it spicy.

VEGETABLE BURGERS WITH CORIANDER CREAM

Vegetable Burgers with Coriander Cream

Ingredients

Burgers:

1 cup red lentils

3 ¼ cups filtered water

2 cups cooked chickpeas, lightly mashed

1 tablespoon fresh ginger, peeled and grated

1 large egg, lightly beaten

1 tablespoon olive oil

1 large onion, diced

Salt and ground black pepper

½ teaspoon ground cumin

¾ cup gluten-free breadcrumbs

¼ cup fresh parsley, finely chopped

¼ cup fresh coriander, finely chopped

1 tablespoon curry powder

additional gluten-free breadcrumbs for coating

macadamia or olive oil for frying

Coriander Cream:

¾ cup raw cashew nuts

½ clove garlic, minced

½ cup filtered water

juice of ½ a lemon

salt to taste

pinch of ground cumin

2 tablespoons fresh coriander, chopped

Method

Burgers:

1. Rinse the lentils and put them in a medium saucepan with the filtered water. Bring the pan to a boil and remove any impurities that rise to the surface. Simmer the lentils until they are tender. Do not let the water reduce; add more if required.
2. In a large bowl, combine the drained lentils with the chickpeas, ginger and egg.
3. Heat the olive oil in a large skillet and sauté the onions until they are soft. Season them with salt, black pepper and the ground cumin.
4. Combine the sautéed onions with the lentil mixture and add the breadcrumbs. Mix well.
5. Add the parsley, coriander and curry powder. Mix well.
6. Divide the mixture into 10 portions and pat them into patties. Gently press each burger into additional breadcrumbs on both sides.
7. Heat the cooking oil in a large skillet and fry each burger until golden brown on each side, approximately 5 minutes. Drain on paper towels before serving.

Coriander Cream:

1. Combine the cashews with the garlic in a blender. Pulse until the nuts are well ground.
2. Add the water, lemon juice, salt and cumin. Process until the mixture is smooth and creamy.
3. Fold in the chopped coriander and serve with the burgers. The coriander cream can also be served with other foods, such as steamed vegetables. Keep if refrigerated in a covered container if you have any leftover or if you make the sauce ahead of time.

Makes 10 | 45 minutes | Freezer-friendly

Nutritional Information:

The combination of lentils and chickpeas makes these high-protein burgers very satiating. A tasty alternative to meat burgers, this is a fantastic way to incorporate more legumes into your diet. They are packed with dietary fibre and a beneficial range of minerals. Serve the burgers with extra greens for a complete meal.

Spelt Pizza with Macadamia Pesto

Spelt Pizza with Macadamia Pesto

Ingredients

Pizza Dough:

2 cups spelt flour

1 teaspoon salt

2 teaspoons (1 packet) baker's yeast

1 tablespoon maple syrup

1 ¼ cups warm filtered water

2 tablespoons olive oil

Pizza Topping:

2 cups pumpkin, peeled and cubed

1 cup sweet potato, peeled and cubed

1 zucchini, sliced

1 tablespoon olive oil

salt and ground black pepper

2 leaves silver beet, stems removed and coarsely chopped

1 cup broccoli florets

¼ cup fresh parsley, finely chopped

1 sprig fresh rosemary, leaves finely chopped

1 sprig fresh thyme, leaves finely chopped

sesame seeds for garnish

Macadamia Pesto:

2 cups basil leaves

1 cup raw macadamia nuts

juice of 1 lemon

salt and ground black pepper

½ cup filtered water

Cheese Sauce:

2 cups raw cashew nuts

1 ½ cups filtered water

2 teaspoons Dijon mustard

2 tablespoons savoury yeast

pinch of turmeric

pinch of salt

Note

Spelt contains gulten.

Tip

Add water to spelt flour gradually until dough forms.

Makes 2 | 60 minutes

Nutritional Information:

This is a fabulous family meal, that is not only tasty but dense with nutrients. Spelt flour is naturally low in gluten and higher in protein than regular white, wheat flour. The pesto coupled with the vegetable topping makes this a great way to tastily increase the plant content of your diet.

Spelt Pizza with Macadamia Pesto

METHOD

PIZZA DOUGH:

1. Combine the spelt flour and salt in a large bowl. Make a well in the centre and pour in the yeast, maple syrup and warm water. Wait for 5 minutes for the yeast to activate.
2. Mix the dough with your hands and knead for about 8 minutes on a lightly floured board.
3. Oil the bowl with half the olive oil. Put the dough in the bowl and coat with the remaining oil. Cover the bowl and let the dough rise while you prepare the rest of the pizza toppings.

PIZZA TOPPING:

1. Preheat the oven to 180°C.
2. Layer the pumpkin, sweet potato and zucchini in a baking dish and toss with oil. Season well and bake for 10 to 20 minutes or until tender.

MACADAMIA PESTO:

1. Combine the basil and macadamia nuts in the bowl of a food processor and grind until the nuts are well chopped and the basil is incorporated.
2. Add the lemon juice and season with salt and pepper.
3. With the motor running, start adding the water. For smooth and creamy sauce, use all the water and blend until the sauce is pureed. For more texture, use less water and don't grind it all the way smooth.

CHEESE SAUCE:

1. Combine all ingredients in a blender. Blend until the sauce is very smooth. Transfer to a squeeze bottle if you have one — this will make it easier to drizzle over the pizzas.

TO ASSEMBLE THE PIZZAS:

1. Lightly flour a work surface. Punch down the risen dough and divide it into 2 balls.
2. Roll each ball into a large circle. Place the dough on an oiled baking tray and use the tines of a fork to dock the dough — that is, stick it randomly all over to prevent it from puffing up too much.
3. Bake the pizza dough for about 8 minutes then remove the trays from the oven.
4. Spread the pizzas equally with the macadamia pesto, then arrange the chopped silver beet over each round. Layer the sweet potato, pumpkin, broccoli and zucchini evenly over each piece.
5. Squeeze or drizzle the nut cheese sauce over each pizza. Sprinkle each one with the chopped parsley, rosemary and thyme.
6. Bake the pizzas another 15 minutes or until the crust is golden brown. Garnish with the sesame seeds.

Lamb Backstrap with Brown Rice Salad and Coconut Raita

Lamb Backstrap with Brown Rice Salad and Coconut Raita

Ingredients

Rice Salad:

1 cup long-grain brown rice

2 cups filtered water

Sprinkle of turmeric

1 small carrot, finely diced

1 spring onion, finely sliced

½ cup red cabbage

⅓ cup peas (fresh or frozen)

1 teaspoon coconut oil

¼ cup buckwheat groats

¼ cup currants

¼ cup fresh coriander, chopped

1 cup diced cucumber

(Add any other vegetables you have available, e.g. snow peas, corn)

1 tablespoon red chilli, seeded and finely chopped (optional)

salt and ground black pepper

Lamb Backstrap:

1 lamb backstrap

2 tablespoons spelt flour

1 tablespoon red chili, seeded and finely chopped

1 clove garlic, minced

¼ cup fresh parsley, finely chopped

2 teaspoons cocnut oil

Coconut Mint Raita Accompaniment:

flesh of 1 young coconut

1 cup raw cashew nuts

¼ cup coconut water

¼ cup filtered water

4 tablespoons lemon juice

2 tablespoon lime juice

1 cup cucumber, finely diced

1 cup mint leaves, finely chopped

1 tablespoon lemon zest, finely grated

salt and ground black pepper

Serves 1-2 | 25 minutes

Note

Spelt contains gulten.

Nutritional Information:

Organic lamb is a rich source of heme iron and zinc. Choose organic, pasture-fed animal protein whenever possible, if you include it in your diet. Served with alkalising greens, this dinner is perfect for those who follow the food-combining concept.

Lamb Backstrap with Brown Rice Salad and Coconut Raita

Method

Rice salad:

1. Cook rice via the absorption method with water and turmeric.
2. Stir-fry carrot, spring onion, cabbage and peas in a small amount of coconut oil until cabbage wilts.
3. Take the pan off the heat and add the rice, buckwheat, currants, fresh coriander and remaining salad ingredients. Season with salt and pepper.

Lamb:

1. In a zip-lock bag combine backstrap with flour, red chili, garlic, parsley and half the oil.
2. Shake the bag until the flour evenly coats the lamb.
3. Heat the remaining coconut oil in a pan and sear lamb for approximately 2–3 minutes each side.
4. Set aside and leave to rest for 5–10 minutes before serving.

Raita:

1. In a good-quality blender blend coconut flesh, cashew nuts, waters and lemon and lime juice until smooth.
2. Finely dice cucumber and chop mint leaves.
3. Fold through lemon zest, cucumber, mint leaves and salt and pepper.

To assemble:

1. Serve sliced lamb backstrap and brown rice salad with raita sauce.

Rice Paper Kelp Noodles with Avocado

Rice Paper Kelp Noodles with Avocado

Ingredients

Noodles:

½ packet kelp noodles

1 bunch fresh mint leaves

½ bunch Thai basil leaves

1 small cucumber, finely sliced

1 cup lettuce, shredded

1 medium carrot, peeled and grated

1 red capsicum, seeded and finely sliced

1 spring onion, finely sliced

salt and ground black pepper

1 packet rice paper rolls

½ avocado, sliced

Dressing:

1 green chili, seeded and finely chopped

juice of 1 large lime

1 ¼ teaspoon maple syrup

1 tablespoon fresh ginger, peeled and grated

1 teaspoon tahini (unhulled if possible)

¼ teaspoon tamari

Dipping Sauce (optional):

1 tablespoon tamari

1 teaspoon fresh ginger, peeled and grated

¼ teaspoon maple syrup

Method

1. Whisk together all the dressing ingredients until they are well combined.
2. Combine the kelp noodles, herb leaves and all the vegetables — except for the avocado — in a large bowl and toss with the dressing. Season with the salt and pepper.
3. Dip each rice paper sheet into a bowl of warm water, then lay it on a plate.
4. Spoon about ⅓ cup of the noodle mixture into the centre of the rice paper. Put 2 slices of the avocado on top of the mixture.
5. Fold the sides into the centre over the filling, and the bottom of the paper up and over. Tuck the bottom of the roll in. Roll from the bottom to the top to form a tight roll.
6. Repeat with each piece of rice paper.
7. Combine all dipping sauce ingredients in a bowl until they are well combined. Serve with rice paper rolls.

Serves 8-10 | 60 minutes

Nutritional Information:

Vegetable rolls are a clever and tasty way of incorporating more vegetables into your diet. They are the perfect finger food for entertaining or as a light summer meal. The kelp noodles ensure you are getting vital iodine. Add a small amount of meat, chicken or fish if that appeals or serve with a pile of green leafy vegetables and more avocado.

Spaghetti Bolognaise with Kelp Noodles

Spaghetti Bolognaise with Kelp Noodles

Ingredients

1 onion, diced
1 clove garlic, minced
500g prime beef mince
400g can tomatoes
2 tablespoons tomato paste
2 tablespoons maple syrup
¼ cup fresh parsley, chopped
¼ cup fresh basil, chopped
1 packet kelp noodles
salt and ground black pepper

Serves 4-5 | 30 minutes

Method

1. Cook onion, garlic, and mince in a pan until softened.
2. Add tomatoes, tomato paste, and maple syrup.
3. Bring to a boil, then reduce heat and simmer until sauce thickens slightly. Add a little water if needed.
4. Just before serving, add fresh parsley and basil and stir through.
5. Place on top of one serving of kelp noodles.

Note

Can also be made with the same proportion of fresh tomatoes as there is tinned. It is advisable to buy your tomatoes in a glass jar whenever possible.

Nutritional Information:

Kelp noodles are a fantastic and nutrient-dense, iodine-rich alternative to pasta. A premium organic mince will provide a significant amount of iron and zinc. Serve with a pile of greens for alkalinity and additional minerals.

Mung Bean Dhal

MUNG BEAN DHAL

INGREDIENTS

5 curry leaves

¼ teaspoon whole cumin seeds

¼ teaspoon yellow mustard seeds

¼ teaspoon garam masala

¼ teaspoon ground cumin

¼ teaspoon fenugreek

1 tablespoon coconut oil

½ large onion, finely diced

1 clove garlic, minced

1 tablespoon fresh ginger, peeled and grated

1 cup dry mung beans

1L filtered water

1 teaspoon salt

1 medium tomato, finely diced

¼ cup fresh coriander, chopped

METHOD

1. Heat a medium saucepan over high heat and add the curry leaves, cumin seeds, mustard seeds, garam masala, ground cumin and fenugreek. Let the spices toast until the seeds pop and the fragrance of all the spices is released. Remove from the heat once this starts to happen.
2. Add the coconut oil to the saucepan. When it is hot, stir in the onion, garlic and ginger. Sauté until they are softened but not brown — you might need to turn down the heat.
3. Add the dry mung beans and the water. Lower the heat to a simmer and let the liquid reduce a little until the mung beans are tender. Season with the salt. Do not allow the water to dry out.
4. Add the diced tomato and the fresh coriander just before serving.

Serves 4-6 | 60 minutes | Freezer-friendly

TIP

Serve with brown rice and coconut yoghurt.

NUTRITIONAL INFORMATION:

The humble-looking mung bean is rich in fibre and high in nutritional value. They have a low glycemic impact, helping avoid a blood-glucose and insulin roller coaster. Dhal is gentle on the digestive system and the warming spices also aid digestive processes.

Lentil and Sweet potato Bake

Lentil and Sweet Potato Bake

Ingredients

Lentils:

2 cups red lentils

3 cups vegetable stock

2 cups filtered water

Vegetables:

1–2 tablespoons olive oil

1 large onion, sliced

1 medium carrot, peeled and diced

1 cup peas (fresh or frozen)

½ cup mushrooms, stemmed and diced

2 celery stalks, diced

1 red capsicum, diced

2 cups fresh parsley leaves, chopped

1 sprig fresh thyme leaves, chopped

2 tablespoons tomato paste

gluten-free breadcrumbs, optional

Sweet Potato Topping:

3 small sweet potato

salt and ground black pepper

Method

Lentils:

1. Rinse the lentils and add them to a large saucepan. Pour in the vegetable stock and water. Bring the pot to a boil and skim off any impurities that rise to the surface. Reduce the heat and simmer until the lentils are soft.
2. Boil the sweet potato until soft. Drain and season them with salt and pepper. Mash them with a fork or wooden spoon and set them aside.

Vegetables:

1. Heat the olive oil in a large saucepan and sauté the onion, carrot, peas, mushrooms, celery and capsicum until softened.
2. Stir in the fresh parsley and thyme, then remove the pan from the heat.
3. Add the sautéed vegetables to the lentils in their cooking liquid. Add the tomato paste and stir until blended.

To assemble:

1. Preheat the oven to 170°C. Spoon the lentil and vegetable mixture into a 30cm x 30cm baking dish.
2. Place the mashed sweet potato on top of the lentil mixture, being careful not to let it sink into the mixture.
3. Sprinkle the gluten-free breadcrumbs over the top, if you are using them. Drizzle the top with a little olive oil and bake for 35 minutes or until heated through.

Serves 4-6 | 70 minutes | Freezer-friendly

Nutritional Information:

This delicious casserole is a fantastic way to incorporate lentils into your diet. They are high in dietary fibre and minerals. Using sweet potato for a mashed starch further lowers the glycemic impact, requiring less insulin to be secreted than a meal with a higher glycemic load. To some, parsley is just for garnish, but it's a highly nutritious green leaf and is my favourite food! Eat more parsley!

Supercharge Stir-Fry

Supercharge Stir-Fry

Ingredients

Stir-Fry:

1 large onion, finely sliced

quarter head
of green cabbage

quarter head of red cabbage

1 head broccoli and its stalk

2 bunches Chinese broccoli

2 zucchinis

500g skinless, boneless chicken thighs

3 kaffir lime leaves, finely sliced

1 teaspoon fresh red chili, finely chopped (optional)

2 tablespoons fresh ginger, finely chopped

1 packet of raw kelp noodles

250g mung beans

1 large bunch fresh coriander, chopped

1 spring onion, finely sliced

4 lime wedges

Light Dressing for Stir-Fry:

1 teaspoon ginger, peeled and grated

¼ cup tamari

1 tablespoon maple syrup

Method

Stir-Fry:

1. Slice onion and other vegetables thinly (even broccoli).
2. On a separate board slice chicken thigh into thin strips.
3. Stir-fry kaffir lime leaves, onion, chili, ginger, and chicken.
4. When chicken is cooked (white in the middle), add remaining vegetables. Stir-fry until cooked, but still slightly crunchy. Add a little water if needed.
5. Add dressing and remove from heat.
6. Add kelp noodles, mung beans, spring onion, coriander and a big wedge of lime before serving.

Dressing:

1. Mix all dressing ingredients in a bowl.

Tip

It is best not to cook kelp noodles due to their high nutrient value. Toss them in at the end so they are warmed but not cooked.

Serves 3-4 | 35 minutes

Nutritional Information:

This stir-fry truly is supercharged. The variety of colour in the recipe is indication of the high nutritional quality. The more colour on your plate, the wider the phytochemical benefit. Phytochemical consumption is considered beneficial in the prevention of chronic diseases such as cancer, stroke, and heart disease. I love the power of greens!

San Choy Bow

San Choy Bow

Ingredients

1 tablespoon macadamia nut oil

½ cup mushrooms, stemmed and chopped

2 medium red chilis, seeded and finely chopped

1 tablespoon fresh ginger, peeled and grated

3 kaffir lime leaves, finely sliced

3 tablespoons tamari

2 tablespoons maple syrup

2 tablespoons sesame oil

¼ cup filtered water

1 ½ cups white quinoa, cooked

1 cup cooked chickpeas

¼ cup fresh coriander, chopped

juice of ½ lime

iceberg lettuce cups

raw macadamia nuts for garnish, optional

Method

1. Heat the macadamia oil in a wok or skillet over medium heat. Do not let the oil smoke.
2. Stir-fry the mushrooms, chili, ginger and kaffir leaves until the fragrance develops, about 2 minutes.
3. Stir in the tamari, maple syrup, sesame oil and about ¼ cup of filtered water.
4. Add the cooked quinoa and the chickpeas and keep stirring.
5. Finish with the fresh coriander and lime juice. Spoon the vegetable mixture into each of the lettuce cups and garnish with chopped macadamia nuts, if desired.

Serves 2-3 | 35 minutes

Nutritional Information:

The combination of quinoa and chickpeas provides an excellent source of protein and dietary fibre as well as an array of nutrients. The protein and the fibre will keep you fuller for longer and the minerals are crucial for muscular function.

African Black-Eyed Beans

African Black-Eyed Beans

Ingredients

1 ½ cups dry black-eyed beans, soaked in water
1.5L filtered water
1 tablespoon macadamia oil
2 stalks celery including leaves, chopped
1 red capsicum, seeded and roughly chopped
¼ teaspoon ground cumin
¼ teaspoon cayenne pepper
1 tablespoon paprika
1 tablespoon maple syrup
pinch of salt
1 ¾ cups coconut milk
1 ¾ cups filtered water
190g tomato paste

Method

1. Drain the beans and put them in a large pot. Cover with fresh water and bring to a boil, the reduce the heat and simmer until tender to the bite.
2. Heat the macadamia oil in a large saucepan and sauté the celery and capsicum. Add the cumin, cayenne, paprika, maple syrup and salt.
3. Add the cooked black-eyed beans to the saucepan. Pour in the coconut milk, water and tomato paste. Stir to blend.
4. Simmer over medium to low heat for about 20 minutes until the beans are tender.

Tip

Serve with cooked brown rice, herbed sour cream and bean shoot sprouts. Slightly spicy, this dish is welcome and warming, for lunch as well as dinner.

Serves 4-6 | 60 minutes | Freezer-friendly

Nutritional Information:

Like most beans, black-eyed beans are high in dietary fibre and potassium. The optimal functioning of cells, tissues and organs in the body is dependent on the correct amount of potassium, which also plays a role in the management of fluid retention.

WITHOUT YOUR HEALTH YOU HAVE NOTHING.
DO NOT LET IT TAKE A HEALTH CRISIS
TO REMIND YOU OF THIS.

— DR LIBBY

Hummus (p.229)

Dressings

Coconut Mint and Coriander Raita (p.221)

Beetroot hummus (p.231)

Tomato Jam (p.225)

Macadamia Nut Pesto (p.223)

Dressings and Condiments

A refreshing and tasty dressing or condiment can give any meal the wow factor. When your food is packed with flavour you are less likely to overeat, looking for more taste. Some people perceive that when choosing healthy options, the flavour and taste of a meal will be compromised.

Conventionally produced condiments and dressings are often laden with poor-quality oils, stabilisers, preservatives and copious amounts of refined sugar and poor-quality salt. The easiest way around this is to make your own! A quick whizz in the blender and they are done. Many of them can be frozen too for later use.

I also wanted to include this section because using dressings and sauces can be another way to amp up the plant content of your diet. The RFC pesto, for example, is packed with green leaves and a flavour that will leave a grin on your face.

The body is truly amazing and it is able to digest and utilise real food. You are doing your body an immense favour by choosing to consume food the way it comes in nature ○.

Raw Satay Sauce

Raw Satay Sauce

Ingredients

1 cup raw cashew nuts, unsalted

¼ cup organic almond butter

2 tablespoons fresh ginger, peeled and grated

1 small fresh red chili, seeded and finely chopped

2 tablespoons tamari

1 tablespoon sesame oil

1 tablespoon maple syrup

¼ cup filtered water

Method

1. Combine the cashew nuts and almond butter in a blender. Pulse until the nuts are fairly well ground.
2. Add the ginger and fresh red chili. Process until the mixture is well blended.
3. Add the tamari, sesame oil and maple syrup to the sauce. Blend well.
4. With the motor running, pour in the water and process until the sauce is a smooth paste.

Tip

Use as a stir-fry sauce for chicken, shrimp and vegetables. It's also delicious as a dipping sauce for vegetables.

Makes 1½ cups | 15 minutes | Freezer-friendly

Nutritional Information:

For those with peanut allergies, you don't have to forgo tasty Asian flavors. This easy-to-make stir-fry sauce has no preservatives, MSG or peanut products. With all the nutrients in the cashews and almonds, this is a healthy, versatile accompaniment to almost any meal.

Cashew Sour Cream

CASHEW SOUR CREAM

INGREDIENTS

1 ½ cups raw cashew nuts

juice of 1 lemon

juice of 1 lime

¾ cup filtered water

pinch of salt

METHOD

1. Combine all the ingredients in a blender. Process until the mixture is smooth.

Makes 2 cups | 15 minutes

NUTRITIONAL INFORMATION:

This refreshing condiment has all the flavour of sour cream but without the unhealthy fats. Use it anywhere you would use sour cream, knowing it contains a range of minerals including calcium and magnesium. It is also rich in heart-healthy monounsaturated fat and contains lemon juice, which your liver loves.

Sweet and Sour Salad Dressing

Sweet and Sour Salad Dressing

Ingredients

2 Medjool dates, pitted and coarsely chopped

2 teaspoons mustard seeds, finely ground

2 teaspoons fresh ginger, peeled and grated

1 teaspoon apple cider vinegar

juice of 1 lemon

juice of 1 orange

2 tablespoons olive oil

salt and ground black pepper

Makes ½ cup | 15 minutes

Method

1. Combine the dates, ground mustard seeds and ginger in a blender. Process until the ingredients are fairly well ground.
2. Add the apple cider vinegar, lemon juice and orange juice. When the mixture is well blended, pour in the olive oil.
3. Season the dressing with salt and black pepper. Keep the dressing covered and chilled until ready to use.

Tip

This dressing is perfect with any salad, especially one with apples or citrus fruits.

Nutritional Information:

Lemon juice, ginger and apple cider vinegar assist with the production of stomach acid and digestive enzymes. Vitamin C-rich lemons are important for immune function and the production of collagen.

Coconut, Mint and Coriander Raita

Coconut, Mint and Coriander Raita

Ingredients

flesh of 1 young coconut

1 cup raw cashew nuts

¼ cup coconut water

¼ cup filtered water

4 tablespoons fresh lemon juice

2 tablespoons fresh lime juice

1 cup cucumber, peeled and finely diced

1 cup mint leaves, finely chopped

1 cup fresh coriander, finely chopped

1 tablespoon lemon zest, finely grated

salt and ground black pepper

Makes 2 cups | 15 minutes

Method

1. Combine the coconut flesh, cashew nuts, filtered and coconut waters, lemon and lime juices in a blender and process until the mixture is smooth.
2. Fold in the cucumber, mint, coriander and lemon zest. Season with salt and pepper. Do not blend the mixture — it is supposed to be slightly chunky.
3. Keep the dressing covered and chilled until ready to use.

Nutritional Information:

The flesh of the young coconut is a good source of dietary fibre, necessary for outstanding gut health. The cashews provide additional minerals such as calcium and magnesium. Gluten- and dairy-free, the cucumber and mint provide a cooling property that is perfect with spicy foods such as curry.

Macadamia Nut Pesto

Macadamia Nut Pesto

Ingredients

2 large cups basil leaves

1 cup raw macadamia nuts

juice of 1 lemon

salt and ground black pepper

½ cup filtered water

Method

1. Combine the basil and macadamias in the bowl of a food processor or blender. Pulse until the nuts are well ground and the basil is well incorporated.
2. With the motor running, add the lemon juice, salt, pepper and enough of the water to make a smooth paste.

Makes 2 cups | 15 minutes

Nutritional Information:

This versatile staple is the quickest and most delicious condiment ever! This no-added-oil recipe features the heart-health benefits of macadamias as well as the highly alkalising effects of the fresh basil and lemon.

Tomato Jam

Ingredients

2 medium-sized tomatoes, roughly chopped

1 small clove garlic, minced

1 teaspoon fresh ginger, peeled and grated

1 small red chili, seeded and finely chopped

¼ cup fresh pineapple, roughly chopped

1 tablespoon coriander root, finely chopped, or finely chopped coriander leaves

¼ teaspoon mustard seeds

2 tablespoons maple syrup

½ cinnamon stick

pinch ground cumin

pinch of dried coriander

salt and ground black pepper

Makes 2 cups | 15 minutes

Method

1. Combine all the ingredients in a medium saucepan and bring to a boil.
2. Reduce the heat and simmer for 5 minutes or until the jam thickens.
3. Remove the cinnamon stick before serving or storing.

Nutritional Information:

Making your own tomato jam eliminates refined sugar, preservatives and artificial colors, plus it tastes so much better! A simple one-pot recipe makes a condiment rich in lycopene, a potent antioxidant found in tomatoes that has proven effective in reducing the risk of prostate cancer.

Red Sauce

Ingredients

1 cup raw cashew nuts

2 Medjool dates, pitted and coarsely chopped

1 medium red capsicum, seeded and chopped

1 small red chili, seeded and finely chopped

juice of 1 ½ lemons

⅓ cup olive oil

Makes 1 cup | 15 minutes

Method

1. Combine the cashews and the dates in a blender. Process until the nuts and dates are fairly well ground.
2. Add the capsicum, chili and lemon juice. Pulse until the ingredients are well blended.
3. With the motor running, pour in the olive oil. Keep the dressing covered and chilled until ready to use.

Tip

Serve with steamed prawns and grilled fish. This sauce gives a snap to omelettes and egg dishes. Perfect as an alternative to cocktail sauce and thousand island dressing.

Nutritional Information:

The vibrant colour of this sauce comes from the fresh capsicum and chili pepper. Capsicums are loaded with vitamin C and beta-carotene, both of which help slow the aging process from the inside out. The cashews add minerals and a lovely texture.

Hummus

Hummus

Ingredients

2 cups sprouted chickpeas

1 large clove garlic, minced

2 ½ teaspoons ground cumin

2 teaspoons tahini (unhulled if possible)

½ cup olive oil

juice of 1 lemon

salt and ground black pepper

Method

1. Combine the chickpeas and garlic in the bowl of a food processor or blender. Pulse a few seconds until the chickpeas are well ground.
2. Add the cumin and tahini to the mixture and pulse until they are well incorporated.
3. With the motor running on low, slowly pour the olive oil into the processor. When the oil has been well blended, add the fresh lemon juice.
4. Season the hummus with salt and black pepper.

Makes 1½ cups | 15 minutes

Nutritional Information:

Sprouting is beneficial for seeds and legumes, as it intensifies their nutrient-density. Chickpeas are a fantastic source of dietary fibre and minerals. Tahini is rich in calcium and magnesium and the olive oil contributes the heart-health benefits of monounsaturated fat. Use this recipe as a base for your hummus, adding spices and herbs as you please. It makes a definite improvement to an ordinary lunchbox and works well as a spread, dip or added source of protein.

Beetroot Hummus

Beetroot Hummus

Ingredients

2 cups sprouted chickpeas

2 whole beetroots, cooked until soft, then peeled and chopped

1 large clove garlic, minced

2 ½ teaspoons ground cumin

2 teaspoons tahini (unhulled if possible)

juice of 1 lemon

½ cup olive oil

salt and ground black pepper

Makes 3 cups | 15 minutes

Method

1. Combine the chickpeas and cooked beetroots in the bowl of a food processor or bender and pulse until the chickpeas are well ground and the beets are fully incorporated.
2. Add the garlic, cumin, tahini and lemon juice. With the motor running, slowly pour in the olive oil and process until it is well incorporated.
3. Season with salt and black pepper.

Tip

Use as a dip for cut-up raw vegetables, such as carrots, celery and zucchini. Halve an avocado and fill the center with the hummus, then sprinkle with a mixture of seeds, such as sesame, poppy, pumpkin and sunflower.

Nutritional Information:

The beets not only give this flavourful hummus its brilliant color, but they aid the liver in detoxifying as well. The garlic enhances the same functions, and the sprouted chickpeas are packed with dietary fibre.

Whole Egg Mayo

Whole Egg Mayo

Ingredients

4 large eggs
1 egg yolk, raw
1 tablespoon apple cider vinegar
1 tablespoon Worcestershire sauce
1 tablespoon maple syrup
1 tablespoon hot mustard
1 tablespoon Dijon mustard
2 ½ to 3 ½ cups olive oil

Makes 1 cup | 15 minutes

Method

1. Soft poach the eggs, cooking for roughly 1 ½ minutes.
2. Add soft-poached eggs to the food processor with one raw egg yolk.
3. Add apple cider vinegar, Worcestershire sauce, maple syrup and mustards.
4. Blend in food processor, adding oil gradually.

Tip

Could also be made into a herbed dressing using dill, mint, capers, etc.

Nutritional Information:

Mayonnaise is traditionally one of the more processed condiments. This is a healthy alternative free from any preservatives, sweeteners, or undesirable vegetable oils. Eggs are a rich source of vitamins A, D and E and they contain a range of B vitamins.

Cashew Cheese Sauce

CASHEW CHEESE SAUCE

INGREDIENTS

2 cups raw cashew nuts

1 ½ cups filtered water

2 teaspoons Dijon mustard

2 tablespoons savoury yeast

pinch of turmeric

pinch of salt

Makes 2 cups | 15 minutes

METHOD

1. Combine the cashew nuts with the water in the bowl of a food processor. Pulse until the nuts are well ground.
2. Add the mustard, yeast, turmeric and salt. Blend until the mixture is smooth.

NUTRITIONAL INFORMATION:

Perfect for steamed cauliflower and other vegetables, this heart-friendly sauce is a tasty alternative to a traditional cheese sauce. Savoury yeast is a good source of B vitamins, essential so the body can extract the energy from food and also for liver detoxification processes.

Tropical Pineapple Chutney

Tropical Pineapple Chutney

Ingredients

6 Medjool dates, pitted and coarsely chopped

¼ cup fresh lemon juice

¼ cup filtered water

½ cup fresh pineapple, finely diced

½ cup desiccated coconut

¼ cup currants

1 tablespoon red onion, finely chopped

1 teaspoon green chili, seeded and finely chopped

½ teaspoon fresh ginger, peeled and grated

¼ cup fresh coriander, chopped

1 teaspoon ground cumin

pinch of salt

Makes 2 cups | 15 minutes

Method

1. Combine the dates, lemon juice and water in the bowl of a food processor or blender. Process until the mixture becomes a smooth paste.
2. Add the remaining ingredients and pulse until the mixture is just blended, not pureed.

Note

Serve this chutney with any grilled or steamed chicken or white fish. Adding a green salad makes this a complete and nutritious meal.

Nutritional Information:

This Caribbean-inspired accompaniment is an excellent source of vitamin C and will add freshness and additional nutrition to any meal. Pineapple contains digestive enzymes, while ginger and cumin also support the digestive process.

Thai Noodle Dressing

Thai Noodle Dressing

Ingredients

1 teaspoon fresh ginger, peeled and grated

1 teaspoon fresh green chili, seeded and finely chopped

1 teaspoon tahini (unhulled if possible)

1 ¼ teaspoons maple syrup

juice of 1 lime

¼ teaspoon tamari or nama shoyu

¼ cup almonds, soaked overnight in water, then rinsed well and chopped

Makes ½ cup | 15 minutes

Method

1. Combine all ingredients in a jar with a tight-fitting lid and shake until well blended. This dressing can also be whisked in a bowl.
2. Keep dressing covered and chilled until ready to use.

Nutritional Information:

An easy way to avoid refined sugars and non-food additives often found in bottled sauces is to make your own sauces and dressings. This sauce delivers all the delicious flavours that are distinct to Asian cuisine. In addition, the tahini is a source of calcium and magnesium, as are the almonds and maple syrup.

Sushi Dressing

Sushi Dressing

Ingredients

1 tablespoon fresh ginger, peeled and grated

1 tablespoon tahini (unhulled if possible)

1 tablespoon rice wine vinegar
or apple cider vinegar

1 ½ teaspoons maple syrup

juice of ½ lemon

Makes ½ cup | 15 minutes

Method

1. Combine all the ingredients in a jar with a tight-fitting lid and shake until the dressing is well blended. This dressing can also be whisked together in a bowl.
2. Keep the dressing covered and chilled until ready to use.

Tip

Use this light and fragrant dressing as a dipping sauce for sushi, with salads or other Asian dishes.

Nutritional Information:

The unique Asian flavours of this sauce come from the tahini and ginger. Tahini is a source of B vitamins, essential for energy and healthy red blood cells. It also contains calcium and magnesium which are great for the nervous system and for muscle contractions. Remember, the heart is a muscle and it loves these nutrients.

A great question to ask yourself before you make a food choice is, "Will this nourish me?" Apply this question to your body, mind and soul.

— Dr Libby

White Chocolate and Blueberry Cake (p.255)

Dessert

Beetroot Chocolate Mud Cake (p.259)

Lemon and Lime Tart (p.251)

Strawberry Cream pie (p.265)

Raw Chocolate Crackle (p.261)

Dessert

I THOUGHT LONG AND HARD ABOUT INCLUDING A SECTION IN MY COOKBOOK ABOUT DESSERTS. MY PHILOSOPHY AND MY MESSAGE WHEN IT COMES TO FOOD IS ABOUT INCREASING THE PLANT CONTENT OF YOUR DIET AND MOST DEFINITELY DECREASING THE REFINED SUGAR. I OFTEN WORK WITH PEOPLE TO DECREASE THEIR RELIANCE ON SUGAR, WHETHER THIS IS IN AN EMOTIONAL CONTEXT OR PURELY PHYSIOLOGICAL. IN MY CLINICAL PRACTICE I HAVE OBSERVED PEOPLE ARE CRAVING SUGAR OR THE SENSATION OF SWEETNESS MORE AND MORE AND UNDOUBTEDLY THIS IS ONE OF THE BY-PRODUCTS OF A NEVER-ENDING TO-DO LIST (DESCRIBED IN DETAIL IN *RUSHING WOMAN'S SYNDROME*), AMOUNG OTHER FACTORS.

In my books I have discussed in detail that at times when people overeat, they aren't looking for food food, they are looking for soul food; and what they are looking for the food to help them feel — well, it never can. Become aware of the why behind your food choices.

I wanted to include a dessert section that offered you an amazing selection that would support your health, rather than take away from it, like most desserts do. I am also aware desserts are sometimes used for celebrations.

If you are going to eat a dessert why not use the most nutrient-dense ingredients that leave you feeling uplifted rather than sluggish and tired? Why not truly celebrate and go all out creating something super-special for a birthday or dinner party? These desserts blow me away every time I look at them and I am so thrilled to share these recipes with you.

The chocolate beetroot cake might just become a staple in your household. With ingredients such as brazil nuts and raw beetroot, it is not going to make your blood glucose soar. It really is so good for you. A stand-out for many will be the homemade chocolates; the rich and velvety flavour of these chocolates will astound you. They are dairy-, gluten- and refined sugar-free and a must for any chocoholic.

Great care has been taken in creating these recipes. The quality of the ingredients has not been compromised.

We have included pure maple syrup as our sweetener because it is vegan-friendly, has a lower fructose component than other sweeteners and contains calcium, magnesium and manganese. Cacao butter is used in place of butter (although I am a fan of organic butter) and cacao powder in place of cocoa. Cacao is the least refined form of cocoa and maintains all the nutritional benefits that are lost in conventional processing. If you cannot find cacao you can use pure, good-quality cocoa although it has a slightly different flavour.

Most of the desserts are based on berries, vanilla or chocolate and all of the flavours are real. Nature doesn't need any assistance!

As with any meal, when it comes to these decadent yet healthy desserts, you need to consider your portion size. Although all of the ingredients are highly nourishing, you may find them quite rich so be in touch with the messages of satiety that come from these special creations. Serve yourself a small piece and savour every mouthful.

Have fun with these recipes. Enjoy the creation process. Some of the cheesecakes look amazing in their own individual ramekins or you may want to end a dinner party with a truffle tower. End your special event on a high, and not of the refined-sugar variety.

Raspberry Macadamia Torte with Chocolate Ganache

Raspberry Macadamia Torte with Chocolate Ganache

Ingredients

Base:

400g raw macadamia nuts

200g sunflower seeds

10 Medjool dates, pitted and coarsely chopped

¾ cup cacao powder

¾ cup desiccated coconut

2 tablespoons filtered water

Ganache and Raspberry Filling:

2 large avocados (flesh only)

10 Medjool dates, pitted and coarsely chopped

¾ cup cacao powder

pinch of salt

3 cups raspberries (fresh or frozen)

Serves 10-12 | 55 minutes

Tip

Excess base ingredients can be used to make nut truffles or energy balls. Roll into balls and freeze for later use. Assembly is for decoration purposes. This can be made into a sandwich or slab style by separating mixture into two portions and filling with ganache and frozen raspberries.

Method

Base:

1. Process all dry base ingredients in a food processor on high until the mixture starts to bind. Add filtered water and continue processing until mixture forms a dough. The mixture should be sticky, and when pressed between your hands it will keep its form.
2. Separate base mixture into three 300g portions.
3. Form portions into balls and roll flat on baking paper. When rolling the mixture out, it should not crumble. If the mixture is crumbling, return to food processor and add another 1 tablespoon of water incrementally until it forms a dough.
4. Roll each portion of dough flat on baking paper to approximately 1cm in thickness. Roll into a square or circle. You can use a 21cm tart tin to get the outline of a perfect circle. Once you have cut your shape, put the excess base aside.
5. Set aside and freeze your three portions of dough while you start to assemble ganache ingredients. Freeze the dough for approximately 20 minutes, so it will hold while assembling.

Ganache:

1. Blend the avocado, dates, cacao, and salt in a food processor until thick and smooth. Stop the food processor and scrape the ingredients down from the sides; continue to process until all ingredients have combined uniformly.

Assembly:

1. Place first frozen base onto a cake plate.
2. Between each layer spread equal amounts of ganache mixture, followed with 1 cup of raspberries. Spread the ganache mixture gently as you don't want the torte to collapse.
3. On the final layer spread the remaining ganache mixture followed by the remaining frozen raspberries for decoration.

Nutritional Information:

Antioxidants galore, calcium, magnesium, zinc... the list of goodness goes on and on! Fancy a torte offering you so much nutrition as well as the yum factor! Enjoy this decadent dessert when you would any other special-occasion cake. Eat it slowly and truly savour every mouthful.

Lemon and Lime Tart

Lemon and Lime Tart

Ingredients

Lemon Lime Filling:

¾ cup coconut oil

2 ½ cups raw cashew nuts

juice of 1 lemon

juice of 2 limes

zest of 2 limes, grated

Base:

6 dried apricots, finely chopped

zest of 1 lime, grated

½ cup raw almonds, soaked overnight, then rinsed well

½ cup desiccated coconut

¼ cup pumpkin seeds

¼ cup white sesame seeds

¼ cup sunflower seeds

¼ cup tahini (unhulled if possible)

½ tablespoon filtered water

Serves 6-8 | 45 minutes

Method

Lemon Lime Filling:

1. Melt the coconut oil in a small saucepan, then allow it to cool.
2. Combine the cashew nuts, lemon and lime juices and lime zest in the bowl of a food processor or blender and pulse until the nuts are well ground.
3. Pour in the coconut oil with the motor running and process until the mixture is smooth and creamy.

Base:

1. Combine the chopped apricots in the bowl of a food processor with the lime zest, almonds, coconut, seeds, tahini and water. Process until the mixture resembles a crumb. If the mixture sticks together when you squeeze it in your hand, it's ready. If it doesn't stay together, add a little more water.
2. Press the base mixture into a 20cm tart pan. A pan with a removable rim would be best.
3. Spread the lemon lime filling evenly over the base and freeze until the filling is firm to touch, about 15 to 20 minutes. Remove the rim if you have a springform pan before serving.

Nutritional Information:

Not only is this delicious tart creamy and light, but lemon juice is a good source of vitamin C and has vital anti-microbial and liver-detoxification properties. The base is a healthier alternative to a regular pastry base, and any leftovers can be rolled into balls and eaten as a snack.

HOMEMADE CHOCOLATES

INGREDIENTS

100g cacao butter

½ cup cacao powder

¼ cup maple syrup

10 drops organic peppermint oil — make sure it is food grade (optional)

¼ cup cacao nibs, for crunch (optional)

METHOD

1. Melt the cacao butter in a small saucepan over low heat, then allow it to cool.
2. Add the maple syrup to the cooled cacao butter, then stir in the cacao powder and mix to blend well.
3. Stir in the drops of peppermint oil if using.
4. Spoon the mixture into ice cube trays and top with the optional cacao nibs. Freeze until set, then pop them out.

Makes 10-12 | 15 minutes

NUTRITIONAL INFORMATION:

There's no compromising the taste when making these homemade chocolates. With no dairy, refined sugar or artificial additives, these amazing chocolates are rich in antioxidants and magnesium. Just one bite will satisfy even the most ardent chocoholic!

White Chocolate and Blueberry Cake

White Chocolate and Blueberry Cheesecake

Ingredients

Base:

¼ cup pumpkin seeds

1 cup raw almonds, soaked overnight, then rinsed well

6 Medjool dates, pitted and coarsely chopped

¼ cup sunflower seeds

¼ cup sesame seeds

½ cup desiccated coconut

⅓ cup tahini (unhulled if possible)

¼ cup cacao nibs

1 tablespoon cacao powder

1 tablespoon filtered water

White Chocolate Filling:

100g cacao butter

½ vanilla bean, split lengthwise and seeds scraped

1 cup raw cashew nuts

¼ cup maple syrup

juice of ½ lemon

Blueberry Filling:

100g cacao butter

1 ½ cup raw cashew nuts

2 punnets fresh blueberries

¼ cup maple syrup

juice of 1 lime

Serves 12-14 | 45 minutes

Nutritional Information:

No wonder this dessert made the cover! Isn't the colour stunning? This is a fantastic alternative to a traditional cheesecake. The nuts and seeds contribute vitamin E and zinc, calcium and magnesium while the blueberries are incredibly high in antioxidants. Cacao butter is the edible fat portion derived from the cacao bean. Big on satiety, this dessert is best served in thin slices.

White Chocolate and Blueberry Cake

METHOD

BASE:

1. Combine the pumpkin seeds, almonds and the chopped dates in the bowl of a food processor. Process until the mixture is well ground.
2. Add the sunflower and sesame seeds, coconut, tahini, cacao nibs and cacao powder. Pulse and add the water, then grind until the base mixture is well combined.

WHITE CHOCOLATE FILLING:

1. Melt the cacao butter in a small saucepan over a low flame. Put the vanilla bean and the seeds in the pan as the butter melts to soften the bean. Let it cool.
2. Combine the cashew nuts, maple syrup and the lemon juice in a blender. Pulse until the nuts are well ground.
3. Remove the piece of vanilla bean, making sure all the seeds are scraped off. Pour the melted butter and vanilla seeds into the cashew mixture and process until smooth and creamy. Remove from the blender and set aside. If the mixture splits add a little water and blend again.

BLUEBERRY FILLING:

1. Melt the cacao butter in a small saucepan over a low flame and allow to cool.
2. Combine the cashew nuts and blueberries in a blender and pulse until the nuts are ground and the blueberries are well incorporated.
3. Add the maple syrup and lime juice, blending well.
4. Pour the melted cacao butter into the mixture and blend until smooth and creamy.

TO ASSEMBLE THE CAKE:

1. Press the base mixture into a 20cm tart pan, preferably one with a removable rim.
2. Pour the white chocolate filling over the base and spread it evenly over the surface, being careful not to blend it in to the base.
3. Freeze for 10 to 15 minutes or until set. When the white chocolate is set, spread the blueberry filling on top.
4. Freeze until the blueberry topping is set, and remove the rim of the tart pan, if you are using a springform pan, before serving.

Beetroot Chocolate Mud Cake

Beetroot Chocolate Mud Cake

Ingredients

Cake Mixture:

2 cups raw brazil nuts

4 Medjool dates, pitted and coarsely chopped

½ cup currants

¼ cup maple syrup

3 medium beetroots, peeled and finely grated

2 cups desiccated coconut

½ cup cacao powder

2 tablespoons psyllium husks, ground

Icing:

100g cacao butter, melted

1 cup raw cashew nuts

½ cup raw cacao powder

½ cup maple syrup

1 teaspoon fresh lemon juice

1 teaspoon tamari

Method

Cake Mixture:

1. Grind the brazil nuts in a food processor, then set them aside in a bowl.
2. Combine the dates, currants and maple syrup in the bowl of the food processor and pulse until smooth.
3. Blend the date mixture with the ground nuts and the grated beetroots in a large bowl.
4. Add the coconut, cacao powder and psyllium husks to the bowl and stir them in until blended with the date and nut mixtures.
5. Scrape the blended mixture back into the bowl of the food processor and pulse until the ingredients are well combined and finely textured.
6. Line a cake tin with baking paper and spread the batter evenly over the bottom. Refrigerate for about 15 minutes or until firm to the touch.

Icing:

1. Gently melt the cacao butter in a small saucepan then allow it to cool.
2. Combine the cashews, cacao powder, maple syrup, lemon juice and tamari in the bowl of a food processor or blender and process until the nuts are well ground.
3. With the motor running, pour in the melted cacao butter and blend until the mixture is smooth.
4. Spoon the icing over the cake and refrigerate until the icing is set, about 15 minutes.

Serves 10-12 | 45 minutes | Freezer-friendly

Nutritional Information:

This cake packs all the divine flavor of a traditional chocolate cake but is so much more beneficial for your health. The beetroot aids in liver-detoxification processes, the psyllium is a great source of dietary fibre and the selenium from the nuts is a potent antioxidant and a nutrient vital for thyroid function. Enjoy in small slices, as these powerhouse ingredients support elimination!

Raw Chocolate Crackle

RAW CHOCOLATE CRACKLE

INGREDIENTS

CRACKLE:

1 cup dehydrated buckwheat groats

¾ cup cacao powder

1 cup desiccated coconut

1 ½ cup currants

¾ cup coconut oil

3 tablespoons maple syrup

FUDGE TOPPING:

8 Medjool dates, pitted and coarsely chopped

½ cup almond meal

¼ cup coconut oil

6 tablespoons cacao powder

METHOD

CRACKLE:

1. To dehydrate the buckwheat groats, spread it out on a baking sheet and set your oven to the lowest it can go. Bake the cereal for 1 hour or until it feels dry and crispy.
2. Combine the buckwheat, cacao powder, coconut and currants in a large bowl, mixing until well blended.
3. Gently heat the coconut oil in a small saucepan over a very low heat until it melts.
4. Pour the oil and maple syrup into the bowl with the dry ingredients and blend it in.
5. Press the mixture into a 31cm baking tin lined with parchment paper or plastic wrap.
6. Freeze until set.

FUDGE TOPPING:

1. Combine the dates and almond meal in the bowl of a food processor and pulse until the dates are well chopped.
2. Melt the remaining coconut oil over a gentle heat. Allow to cool. Move the date and almond mixture to a bowl and add the cacao powder and cooled coconut oil. Massage the mixture with your hands until it begins to bind.
3. Press the icing evenly over the frozen crackle. Smooth it with hands and fingers, then return it to the freezer to set the topping.

Makes 10-12 slices | 25 minutes | Freezer-friendly

NUTRITIONAL INFORMATION:

Buckwheat consumption has been linked to lowered levels of cholesterol as well as containing tryptophan, an amino acid precursor to serotonin, the "happy hormone". Rich in magnesium and antioxidants, this delicious dessert is gluten- and dairy-free, and perfect in small bites.

Chocolate Mint Slice

Chocolate Mint Slice

Ingredients

Base:

2 cups raw almonds, soaked in water

6 Medjool dates, pitted and coarsely chopped

1 cup cacao powder

½ cup desiccated coconut

1 to 2 tablespoons tahini (unhulled if possible)

2 tablespoons filtered water

Mint Chocolate Layer:

1 tablespoon Spirulina powder/ green powder

10 drops peppermint oil

2 cups raw cashew nuts

½ cup filtered water

¼ cup maple syrup

Chocolate Icing:

2 cups raw cashew nuts

½ cup maple syrup

¾ cup cacao powder

½ cup filtered water

100g cacao butter

¼ teaspoon tamari

Method

Base:

1. Blend all base ingredients in a food processor until combined.
2. Press into a 25cm x 35cm slice tin.
3. Freeze for 10–15 minutes or until set.

Mint Chocolate Layer:

1. Blend all ingredients in a blender until smooth.

Chocolate Icing:

1. Melt cacao butter in a small saucepan over gentle heat.
2. Allow to cool.
3. Combine all ingredients in a blender and blend until smooth.

Assembly:

1. Spread mint chocolate layer evenly over base mixture.
2. Once spread evenly over base, allow to set in the freezer.
3. Once the mint layer has set (or is firm to the touch), spread chocolate icing layer over and return to freezer until chocolate icing is firm to the touch.

Makes 10-12 slices | 30 minutes | Freezer-friendly

Nutritional Information:

Almonds, cacao, coconut, cashews, tahini, spirulina... wow! What a nutrient-dense line-up in this delicious dessert. Not only does it look pretty, your taste buds and the cells of your body will be very glad you made it. Very satisfying due to the healthy fat content, a small piece will hit the spot!

Strawberry Cream Pie

Strawberry Cream Pie

Ingredients

Base:

zest of one lime

6 dried apricots, chopped

¼ cup sunflower seeds

¼ cup pumpkin seeds

¼ cup sesame seeds

½ cup almonds, soaked overnight, then rinsed well

½ cup desiccated coconut

¼ cup tahini (unhulled if possible)

½ tablespoon filtered water

Strawberry cream filling:

100g cacao butter

2 ½ cups raw cashew nuts

2 ½ centimetres of vanilla stick

½ cup maple syrup

juice of 1 lime

2 punnets fresh strawberries

Method

Base:

1. Add all base ingredients to a food processor and blend until it forms a crumb.
2. Press the dough between your fingers to check that it will stick together.
3. Line a 20cm tart tin with base mixture by pressing in with your fingers.

Strawberry Cream Pie Filling:

1. In a small saucepan, melt cacao butter. Allow it to cool.
2. In a blender, blend cacao butter, cashews, vanilla, maple syrup, lime juice, and strawberries until smooth.

Assembly:

1. Pour strawberry cream pie filling onto your base mixture.
2. Spread evenly with a spatula to achieve an even surface.
3. Freeze until it is firm to the touch.

Serves 8-10 | 40 minutes | Freezer-friendly

Nutritional Information:

This strawberry delight is a gluten-free and dairy-free alternative to strawberry cheesecake. Isn't the colour glorious? Fresh summer strawberries are a good source of vitamin C, coupled with a base packed with nutrients your brain will love. If you have an allergy to strawberries, blueberries can be substituted. Serve yourself a small slice and savour every bite.

Orange Chocolate Tart

Orange Chocolate Tart

Ingredients

Base:

1 cup raw walnuts

½ cup desiccated coconut

¼ cup cacao powder

¼ cup cacao nibs

5 Medjool dates, pitted and coarsely chopped

1 tablespoon tahini (unhulled if possible)

½ tablespoon filtered water

Orange chocolate filling:

100g cacao butter

2 ½ cups raw cashew nuts

2 oranges, rinds and juice

½ cup maple syrup

¾ cup cacao powder

Method

Base:

1. Blend all base ingredients until a fine crumb is formed.
2. Press evenly into a small tart tin (23cm round) or alternatively a slice tin (18cm x 28cm pan).

Filling:

1. In a small saucepan on low heat, melt cacao butter and allow to cool.
2. In a blender combine all filling ingredients until smooth.

Assembly:

1. Spread orange chocolate mixture evenly over base mixture.
2. Use a spatula to achieve an even surface.
3. Place in freezer until chocolate filling is firm to touch.

Tip

This mixture can also be used to make an orange chocolate slice. Set the base in a slice tin and cover with orange chocolate mixture. Alternatively the orange chocolate mixture can be used to form chocolate without the base mixture.

Serves 8-10 | 45 minutes | Freezer-friendly

Nutritional Information:

An all-time favourite, this orange chocolate delight packs a nutritional punch. It is not often that cakes contain omega-3, magnesium and calcium. Enjoy a small slice and know you are doing your nutrient levels a great big favour!

Omega Oil Chocolate Sauce

Omega Oil Chocolate Sauce

Ingredients

½ cup macadamia oil
(Udo's oil or high-quality flax oil)

½ teaspoon vanilla extract

1 cup maple syrup

1 cup cacao powder

pinch of salt

Makes 1½ cups | 15 minutes

Method

1. Blend all ingredients in a blender until smooth.
2. Serve on top of berries or fresh pineapple, banana and coconut.

Nutritional Information:

Getting children to have their omega-3 oil can be difficult, but not when it tastes like a velvety chocolate sauce. A great way of eating Udo's oil or simply as an alternative to a highly processed food, this sauce is lovely served with a fist-sized serving of berries or fresh fruit.

Essentials for Pantry

Dry Goods

Nuts
Almond butter
Peanut butter
Raw cashews
Raw almonds
Raw brazil nuts
Raw macadamias
Raw walnuts

Seeds
Sunflower seeds
Pumpkin seeds
Flaxseeds (linseeds)
Black sesame seeds
White sesame seeds

Grains, lentils and legumes
Quinoa —
black, red and white
Brown rice
Red rice
Black rice
Red lentils
Green split peas
Brown lentils
Puy lentils
Mungbeans
Chickpeas
Black-eyed peas

Flours
Spelt flour
Amaranth flour
Quinoa flour
Buckwheat flour

Spices and Salts
In the RFC recipes, when we list salt as an ingredient, we are referring to: Celtic sea salt and/or Himalayan salt (make sure the brand you buy contains iodine)

Black whole peppercorns
Cumin seeds
Caraway seeds
Coriander seeds
Mustard seeds
Celery seeds
Garam masala
Curry powder
Cayenne pepper
Sweet paprika
Nutmeg
Cinnamon
Cardamom
Star anise
Vanilla bean
Good-quality vanilla extract
Peppermint oil
Saffron

Sweetners
Pure maple syrup

Dried Fruits
Make sure you buy dried fruit with no added preservatives.

Medjool dates
Apricots
Currants
Sultanas
Prunes

Oils/Fats
Extra-virgin olive oil
Coconut oil
Macadamia oil
Avocado oil
Flaxseed oil
Cacao butter
Organic butter

Bottled/Pre-packaged items
Coconut milk
Coconut cream
Tomatoes
Tomato paste
Dijon mustard
Hot mustard
Balsamic vinegar
White wine vinegar
Apple cider vinegar

Other Items
Desiccated Coconut (make sure you choose a preservative free brand)
Coconut (chips or flakes)
Cacao Powder
Cacao nips
Dehydrated buckwheat
Baking powder (aluminium free)
Baking Soda (aluminium free)

Fridge list

Vegetables
Cucumber
Kale
Spinach
Silverbeet
Brocolli
Pumpkin
Sweet potato
Potato
Carrots
Corn
Peppers (all colours)
Onion
Red Onion
Fresh ginger
Fresh garlic

Fresh Herbs
Lemongrass
Flat-leaf parsely
Coriander
Thyme
Mint
Basil
Chili

Fruit
Tomato
Avocado
Bananas
Blueberries
Raspberries
Passionfruit
Mango (if in season)

Real Food Storage

Storage

When food is made from real ingredients it lacks preservatives to keep it fresh. Real food decomposes—it is supposed to. Here is a guide to storing your sweet food.

Drinks

All of the drinks are best consumed on the day. Nut milk and nut milk-based drinks can be kept in the fridge for two to three days. Juices and smoothies are best consumed straight after making for nutrient retention. They won't spoil over the day so you can drink them later if you prefer.

Sauces

All of the sauces can be stored safely in the fridge for five to seven days, or frozen for three to four months.

Raw Snacks and Desserts

Raw snacks and desserts made with fresh fruit or nuts can be stored in the fridge for four to six days or frozen for three to four months.

Baked Snacks and Desserts

Baked snacks and desserts can be stored in an airtight container for three to four days or frozen for three to four months.

Real Food Chef Glossary

Almond butter: Made from whole raw almonds ground with or without salt to produce a paste. Used to add a nutty flavour to our raw satay sauce.

Amaranth flour: High in the amino acid lysine, amaranth flour adds sweetness and moisture to baked goods when ground into flour. It is gluten-free.

Apple cider vinegar: Can be used in place of any vinegar. It helps to stimulate stomach acid production.

Avocado oil: Pure avocado oil has a high smoke point and is a good source of the protective monounsaturated fats.

Brown rice: Is a whole grain and is also gluten-free. Unpolished whole natural brown rice is higher in minerals, protein and flavour than white rice.

Cacao butter: The fat portion of the cacao bean provides the melt-in-your-mouth texture.
It is a vegan source of fat.

Cacao nibs: A rich source of minerals such as magnesium and iron. The nibs add texture to baking and have a very high antioxidant value.

Cacao powder: The rawest form of chocolate, it maintains the nutrients that are destroyed by conventional processing. It is high in tryptophan which can help enhance mood. If you cannot find it you can substitute it for a high-quality, pure cocoa powder.

Cashews: A good source of magnesium and healthy fats, cashews are a welcome addition to many sauces and dairy alternatives. They add a wonderful creamy texture to dishes.

Celtic sea salt: Comes from the ocean and is less refined than table salt. High in trace minerals, it contains no chemicals. Many brands have been fortified with iodine.

Chickpeas: A legume that needs to be soaked in water before being cooked in fresh water. A good source of protein and fibre. Used to make hummus or can be a nutrient-rich addition to any meal or salad.

Coconut oil: Coconut oil is rich in short and medium chain fatty acids, namely lauric acid, which is also found in breast milk. The virgin organic oil has a mild coconut favor that comes through in baked goods. It stays solid at room temperature and has an extremely long shelf life. Can also be used as a skin moisturiser. Very stable in cooking.

Flaxseed oil: A great source of anti-inflammatory omega-3 fatty acids, of particular importance for vegans or vegetarians. Never heat flaxseed oil. Drizzle it over the top of salads or vegetables, or add to smoothies. Always buy a reputable brand and use the bottle within 6 weeks of opening. This oil oxidises (goes rancid) easily and is best consumed with a source of vitamin C and/or E.

Galangal: Is part of the ginger family and found in Asian grocery stores. Has a very distinctive flavour and is a key component to many Thai dishes.

Kale: Part of the Brassica family, kale is a leafy green containing the cancer-fighting sulforaphane. Can be used in place of or as well as silver beet or spinach.

KELP NOODLES: Made from kelp, these noodles are gluten-free, dairy-free and a source of iodine. A nutrient-dense and real food alternative to other noodle options. A raw food.

LEMONGRASS: Has a subtle citrus flavor enhanced by bruising it before using it. It may have anti-fungal properties.

MACADAMIA OIL: Has a high smoke point making it suitable for use in cooking as well as raw dishes. A good source of monounsaturated fats, it has a light, nutty flavour.

MAPLE SYRUP: A sweetener that is an ideal replacement for refined sugar. It contains small amounts of calcium, magnesium and manganese.

MEDJOOL DATES: Provide moisture and sweetness to a number of our recipes. High in fibre and potassium and also a source of iron. Often found in the fresh section of supermarkets and organic stores.

MUNG BEANS: Used in place of lentils for our dhal, they can also be sprouted and used in salads.

QUINOA: Is considered a grain even though it is actually a small seed. It has a mild nutty flavour and is gluten-free. It is one of the only complete plant proteins meaning it contains all essential amino acids.

RED LENTILS: Used in soups and dhal and is a great source of protein and fibre.

SAVOURY YEAST/NUTRITIONAL YEAST: Is a combination of vitamins and inactive yeast that produces a cheesy/nutty flavour. Not to be confused with brewer's yeast or active yeast.

SPELT FLOUR: Considered an ancient grain, spelt is closer to the original form of wheat humans consumed. Those sensitive to wheat can sometimes tolerate spelt. Contains gluten so not suitable for people with celiac disease.

SPROUTS: Seeds and grains can be sprouted and added to snacks, salads or any meal. They are rich in enzymes, vitamins and minerals.

TAHINI: Is a seed butter made from ground sesame seeds. It has a distinctive sesame flavour and is a delicious addition to dressings, baking and meals. Rich in calcium.

TAMARI: Is traditionally made soy sauce. Most varieties are wheat-free but it pays to read the label.

TAMARIND PASTE: Sweet and sour in taste and available from health food stores or Asian grocery stores. Made from tamarind, this provides the distinctive flavour in our Pad Thai sauce.

TRICOLOURED QUINOA: Red, black and white quinoa in dry form. Looks attractive and is often used in salads. Can be replaced with white quinoa.

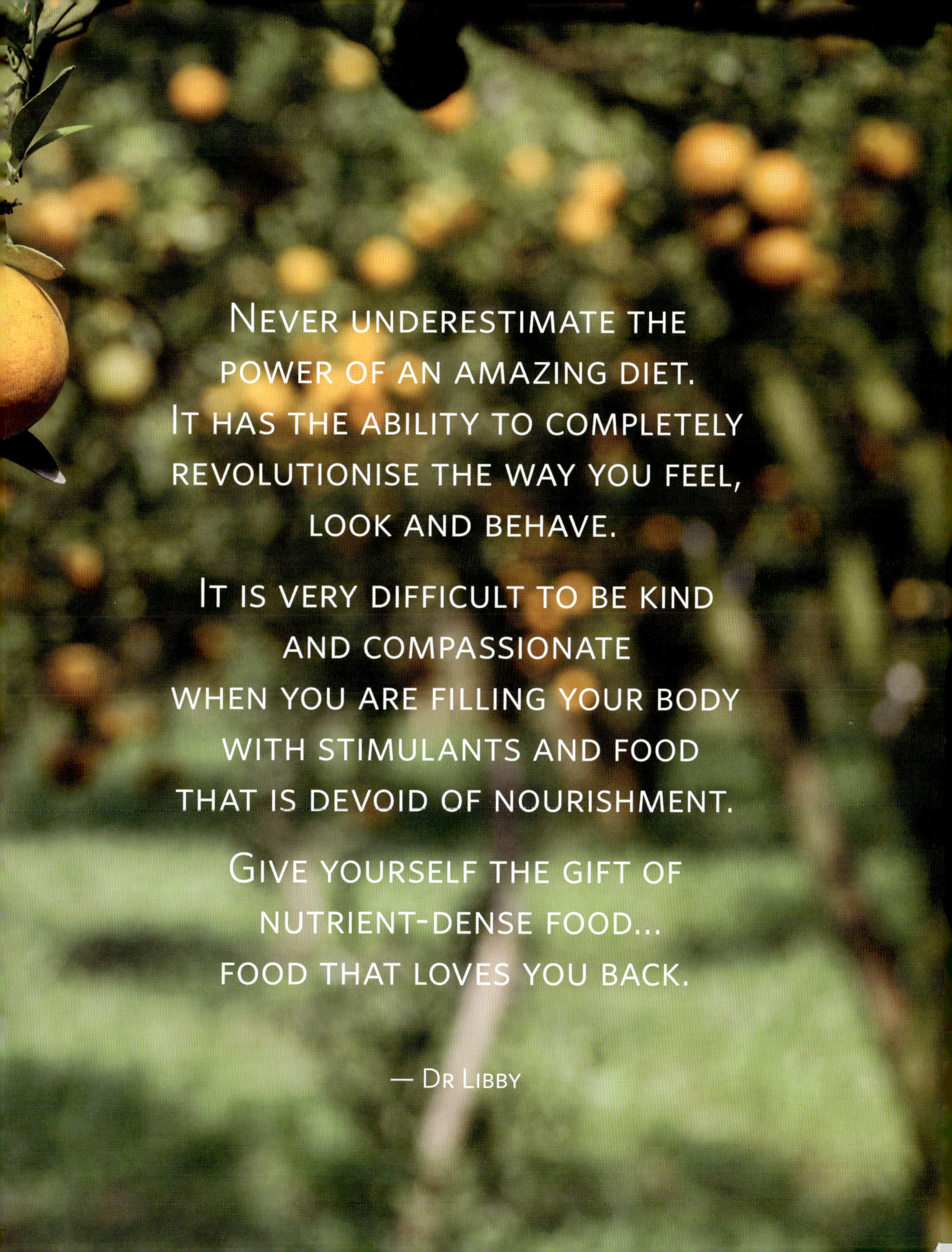

Never underestimate the
power of an amazing diet.
It has the ability to completely
revolutionise the way you feel,
look and behave.

It is very difficult to be kind
and compassionate
when you are filling your body
with stimulants and food
that is devoid of nourishment.

Give yourself the gift of
nutrient-dense food...
food that loves you back.

— Dr Libby

Acknowledgements

The creation of this cookbook has well and truly been a team project. Firstly, to the incredibly talented and passionate Chef Cynthia Louise for her extraordinary creations. We sat together and designed what Real Food is all about. Food that is not only made with ingredients the way they come in nature but food that can be created simply and that whole families can enjoy. Thank you for using measuring cups (!!) so we could create recipes from your creations but even more so for the love and care that radiates from your food. I am so thrilled the world can now experience your gifts.

Massive thanks to Nicole Rayment, our gorgeous production manager, for your meticulous attention to detail and exceptional time management. Thanks Nic. To Gavin Johns, for his magnificent photography and humour and to the team at Red Rocket Studios, Sydney for the use of their wonderful space.

To Sven Lowe for your extraordinary talent, creative flair and for keeping Chef Cynthia Louise on schedule, playfully. Your calm is much appreciated.

To Kate. Huge heartfelt gratitude for your dedication to and excitement about this project. Thank you for capturing not only the physical recipes but also their essence. And thanks for your nutrition knowledge, for taste-testing all of the recipes and for your passion for Real Food. And thanks to Imogen for helping spread the message of what Real Food is all about and to Jenny for sharing the power of outstanding nutrition through individual consultations and her deep level of care for people.

Thanks to Joan McKenzie for your advice and guidance. It is much appreciated. To Stasia, thank you so, so much for your layout and design skills and for working so calmly to deadlines! Thanks to Phil and the team at Image Centre for your wisdom and guidance from the printing world.

Huge thanks to the very kind Brent and Wendy for your input in the final stages of this manuscript. And to Garry Kewish for his ongoing insight and support. It is invaluable.

To my dear mum and dad. Thank you for the way you raised me and for loving me unconditionally. Mum, thank you for being the kindest lady on the planet and for teaching me so much about the fundamentals of good nutrition. Dad, thanks for letting me raise chickens and grow parsley in the backyard.

To all of the farmers and producers for their hard work and care in growing organic produce. To the independent producers who are motivated to provide Real Food of the highest quality. We have a choice when we buy our food and it is my hope that more people will choose to support you and encourage manufacturers to consider what they use when producing food.

And so, so importantly, to my dearest Chris. This entire project could never have happened without you. My deepest thanks for your unwavering belief and guidance on this project and for reminding us girls what "real" people want in a recipe and for ensuring the hashbrowns are up to scratch. You rock my world.

Dr Libby Weaver

September, 2012

Meet Dr Libby

Some people have a unique and contagious effervescence about them; an X-factor that compels you to want to be around them; a magnetism that evokes a desire to share in their knowledge; and an energy that, of its own accord, truly inspires and motivates. Dr Libby, PhD is one such person.

Dr Libby Weaver is one of Australasia's leading nutritional biochemists, authors and speakers. With an extraordinary ability to relate to all demographics, from all walks of life, Dr Libby is a dynamic and highly experienced presenter, who can successfully educate nine people in a boardroom or 9000 people on a stage alongside America's Dr Oz.

She is a seven-time number-one bestselling author of the books *Accidentally Overweight, Rushing Woman's Syndrome, Real Food Chef, Beauty from the Inside Out, Real Food Kitchen, The Calorie Fallacy and Sweet Food Story.*

With a background in biochemistry and a natural ability to break down even the most complex of concepts into layman's terms, Dr Libby's health messages are globally relevant, which is why her holistic approach and unique form of education is embraced by audiences across the world.

Her PhD examined biochemical and nutritional factors in children with autism, and her findings have since changed the way the condition is treated in Australia and New Zealand.

Armed with abundant knowledge, scientific research and a true desire to help others get back in touch with how amazing they are, Dr Libby empowers and inspires people to take charge of their health and happiness. Her knowledge and nutritional philosophy is brought to life in her books and cookbooks.

It's no surprise when it comes to health, Deborra-lee and Hugh Jackman described her as a "one-stop shop in achieving and maintaining ultimate health and wellbeing".

Meet Chef Cynthia Louise

Chef Cynthia Louise completed her formal chef's training at a leading health retreat in the Gold Coast hinterland, Australia. Her work focuses on real, whole foods, food as nature intended, that are then transformed into dishes that appeal to everyone. Chef Cynthia Louise then found her calling working with people individually, helping them to create simple dishes that their entire family will enjoy.

She has worked alongside Dr Libby for a number of years, sharing her desire to educate and inspire, and assisting people, from cancer suffers to people with allergies, to deal with a variety of nutritional requirements. Chef Cynthia Louise's true passion lies in the simple act of helping people create stress-free and simple dishes that taste wonderful and that serve the whole body.

Chef Cynthia Louise owned a restaurant that specialised in whole foods that was vegan and gluten-, caffeine- and refined sugar-free. Here she also began her passion for teaching by offering cooking classes, consulting to restaurants and providing coaching to individuals seeking guidance in their Real-Food journey. She also travels the world as a specialist retreat chef and uses these journeys to learn from local cuisines.

Chef Cynthia Louise currently lives in Bali, creating new recipes, supporting people's health, and sharing her passion and gifts. Her food makes achieving optimal health simple and delicious. Chef Cynthia Louise's mission is to ignite people's passion and taste buds, and to teach people how to prepare and cook meals and snacks the whole-foods way.

ACCIDENTALLY OVERWEIGHT

ACCIDENTALLY OVERWEIGHT, DR LIBBY'S FIRST NUMBER-ONE BESTSELLING BOOK, EXPLAINS WHAT IS NECESSARY FOR THE BODY TO BE ABLE TO ACCESS BODY FAT AND BURN IT. SO MANY READERS SAY THAT *ACCIDENTALLY OVERWEIGHT* COULD EASILY BE CALLED "OPTIMAL WELLBEING", AS THE INFORMATION IS RELEVANT TO EVERYONE REGARDLESS OF THEIR HEALTH GOALS.

Whether consciously or subconsciously, many people are frustrated by how they feel about their body, including sometimes its appearance, and this frustration can take up their headspace and influence their moods. Many people eat well and exercise regularly, yet their body fat does not reflect their efforts. This book explains the biochemistry and emotions of weight loss to help free people from their battle with their bodies. It includes strategies to explore emotional eating and specific herbs and nutrients to support optimal biochemistry for the effective utilisation of body fat.

What to eat and how much to eat for optimum health and ideal body shape and size can seem like confusing and, at times, overwhelming areas to explore. Right now you could walk into a bookshop and pick up a book that tells you to eat plenty of carbohydrates, as they are essential for energy, and right beside it on the bookshelf will be a book that tells you not to eat carbs because they make you fat and tired.

How on Earth are you supposed to make sense of this well-meaning, but conflicting, information? How do you work out a way of eating that fuels you with great energy all day long while burning fat? What do you do if you feel like you have tried everything to lose weight only to gain it back? Have you ever put your mind to losing weight and made an enormous effort to eat well and exercise regularly for little or no reward? Or perhaps you are actually OK with your weight but you just don't feel right? *Accidentally Overweight* answers all of these questions, and more.

TO LEARN MORE, VISIT WWW.DRLIBBY.COM

Rushing Woman's Syndrome

Hot on the heels of Dr Libby's first number-one bestselling book, *Accidentally Overweight,* her second book, *Rushing Woman's Syndrome,* became another number-one bestseller. *Rushing Woman's Syndrome* describes the biochemical and emotional effects of constantly being in a rush, and the health consequences that urgency elicits.

It doesn't seem to matter if a woman has two things to do in her day or 200; she is in a pressing rush to do it all. She is often wound up like a top, running herself ragged in a daily battle to keep up. There is always so much to do, and she rarely feels like she is in control and on top of things. In fact, her deep desire to control even the smaller details of life can leave her feeling out of control, even of her own self.

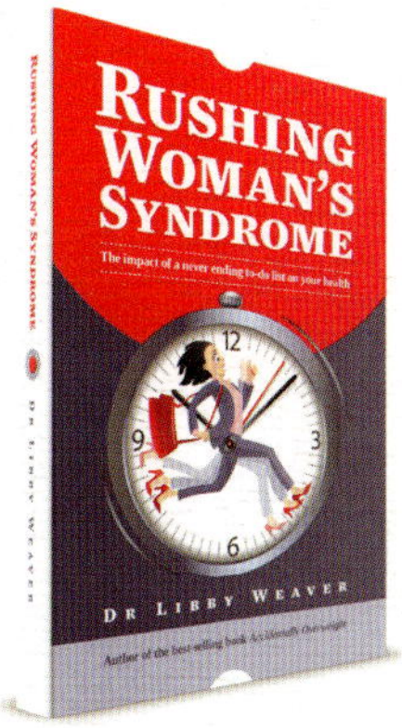

Rushing Woman's Syndrome examines the nervous system, endocrine system (including sex and stress hormones, the thyroid, and the pituitary gland), and the digestive system, as well as the emotional aspects of why women rush. Dr Libby can simplify even the most difficult biochemistry effortlessly, making this book equally educating and inspiring. What sets Dr Libby's work apart in a world where we are constantly bombarded with health messages, is her ability to search for, and explain, the underlying cause of an ailment, the why. *Rushing Woman's Syndrome* takes you on an emotional journey to help you decipher just where your beliefs are coming from and how those thoughts affect how your body behaves. So come on a journey of food and hormones, thoughts and perceptions, energy, and vitality. It is impossible not to see your life and body from a whole new perspective after reading this book.

Rushing Woman's Syndrome was inspired by Dr Libby's clinical experiences and her empathy for women and the many roles they now juggle.

Dr Libby believes we have to be educated and inspired to make changes; her unique conversational style makes you feel like she is speaking right to you. In the book, Dr Libby combines two decades of personal experience, 14 years of university, and 15 years of clinical experience in this book, to offer you real solutions to both the biochemistry and the emotional patterns of the rush.

After a multitude of requests for coaching and requests from women who were too busy to read the book (!), Dr Libby created two 30-day video coaching programmes called *The Rushing Woman's Syndrome Quick Start Course* and the *Condition the Calm Advanced Course*, which guide you on your journey from rushing back to calm. These courses have achieved phenomenal results with women across the world who are now enjoying life without the rush.

To learn more, visit www.drlibby.com

Beauty from the Inside Out

As a society our relationship with beauty is in crisis. We are told that beauty exists only in certain forms, images and at certain ages. We can feel bombarded with images that lead us away from our own unique beauty and encourage us to try to look like someone else rather than accepting more of who we are.

While adults can be affected by such messages, these messages can be particularly damaging to children and teenagers who so desperately want to be loved, approved of, considered special and seen as beautiful. There is so much beauty on offer to us 24/7, at any age, inside us, around us, and shining from us. For so many a veil just needs to be lifted so you can experience your own radiance. Let's see what we can do!

When most people think about improving their appearance, they usually focus on a product, another "quick fix". Yet when you consider that the skin cells on your face are a small percentage of the total number of cells in the whole body, it seems crazy that we don't spend more time getting the majority of the cells functioning optimally, leading us to the outcomes we seek.

Through *Beauty from the Inside Out*, Dr Libby expertly explains your outer world, the food you choose, the nutrients you ingest, hydration, posture, movement and what your body needs to create lovely nails, lustrous hair, sparkling eyes, and clear, luminous skin. Be guided to deal with very specific bumps in the road, such as dark circles under the eyes, eczema, pimples, and hair that is falling out, to name only a few. Just as importantly, Dr Libby explains your inner world, sex hormones, stress hormones, detox, digestion, elimination pathways, thyroid and pituitary functions. Both worlds relate to your sparkle. In addition, taking a heart-opening look at your emotional landscape is important because, for many, that is where the real elixir is.

Beauty from the Inside Out is a must-have beauty bible for all women. Enjoy radiating your own unique sparkle, from the inside out. Dr Libby has also released an online course called Dr Libby's *Essential Beauty Gems.*

To learn more, visit www.drlibby.com

The Calorie Fallacy

How many of us have been told that if we burn more calories than we eat, weight loss will be inevitable? How many of us have discovered that this century-old philosophy does not seem to apply to our body no matter how hard we work, in this modern world?

In a world obsessed with calorie counting, as evidenced by the widespread listing of calories on food items and menus, claims of the latest low-calorie miracle food, diet, and exercise regime guaranteed to burn calories fast, we find ourselves instead watching the waistlines of the Western world continually increasing.

What if the foundation nutritional philosophy that the calorie equation is the sole determinant of weight loss is completely outdated and in many cases wrong?

Bestselling author Dr Libby's book *The Calorie Fallacy* is designed to help you stop dieting and start living. It is time to stop counting calories. It's time for a new model of how to manage body shape and size. No longer are energy equations satisfactory in the information they provide. The concept that as long as you eat fewer calories than you burn you will lose weight is well overdue for an update.

Dr Libby explores the fundamentals of weight loss like never before in this groundbreaking book, that challenges the very core of weight-loss convention and dogma. Through sharing her own personal story and the journey that set her on to uncover and explore the biochemistry of sustainable weight loss, Dr Libby shares countless case studies of clients she has worked with over the past 16 years, along with her two decades of scientific research into the principles of body-fat loss.

Dr Libby contests the assumption that you have to lose weight to be healthy, instead replacing it with a paradigm-shifting statement that in fact you have to be healthy to lose weight. This will transform how you view your body and enhance your understanding of what your body requires to lose weight.

So for all of you who have been making an enormous effort and commitment to weight loss with little or no sustainable outcomes, and for those who simply want to understand how to live happier, healthier lives, allowing your body to efficiently use body fat as a fuel, Dr Libby will arm you with the wisdom to stop dieting and depriving yourself and start thriving. Stop dieting and start nourishing yourself and watch the transformation occur.

Dr Libby's Real Food Kitchen

FOLLOWING ON FROM THE PHENOMENAL SUCCESS OF THE *REAL FOOD CHEF*, THE SECOND COOKBOOK IN THIS SERIES TAKES FAMILY FAVOURITES AND APPLIES THE *REAL FOOD CHEF* PRINCIPLES TO ENSURE MAXIMUM NUTRIENT DENSITY OF EVERY MEAL AND EVERY MOUTHFUL.

With 90 recipes covering breakfast, drinks, lunch, dinner, snacks, dressing and desserts, the *Real Food Kitchen* will inspire you to take better care of yourself with the delicious and nutritious recipes featured.

This way of eating has a wide-reaching effect for it is not just about the outstanding nourishment that comes from each recipe, it is also about what we've left out... refined and artificial ingredients that have the potential to take away from your health such as refined sugar, white flour and preservatives.

This book provides you with amazing recipes such as Macho Nachos, Coconut Ice, Caramel Slice and Banoffee Pie that serve your health and happiness, and brings it all to life in an easy-to-use, quick-to-prepare, and delicious-tasting recipe system. Continue your journey to outstanding health, energy, and vitality by embracing the *Real Food Kitchen* way of eating, and witness the transformation as your body, mind and soul respond to true nourishment.

TO LEARN MORE, VISIT WWW.DRLIBBY.COM

Dr Libby's Sweet Food Story

Countless people make great food choices for breakfast and lunch and then at 3 o'clock in the afternoon or after dinner, they feel like someone else has taken over their body. The desire for and subsequent consumption of sweet food can take hold without you really knowing why or what to do about it.

Too many people reach for sweet food that doesn't serve their health; in fact it may contain substances that actually have the potential to take away from their health, yet they feel powerless to live any differently, having "tried" to change their sweet food habits many times.

Dr Libby clearly explains the sugar conundrum, how the body uses sweet foods and ingredients, and why you may crave them. Dr Libby's *Sweet Food Story* also explains the biochemical pathways involved in the digestion, absorption and utilisation of sweet foods. The book provides you with recipes that offer practical and very delicious ways to enjoy sweet foods made from real-food ingredients.

This book is essential reading for everyone particular those with a sweet tooth. Dr Libby offers you delicious ways to enjoy sweet food while nourishing your body in the best way possible.

To learn more, visit www.drlibby.com

Notes

Notes

Notes